Epic Journey

EPIC JOURNEY

Boundless Dharma

JUSTIN BREEN

amplify

www.amplifypublishinggroup.com

Epic Journey: Boundless Dharma

Conceptual Art Design: Alexandra Tanner and Liam Nacson

For more information, please contact:
Amplify Publishing, an imprint of Amplify Publishing Group
620 Herndon Parkway, Suite 220
Herndon, VA 20170
info@amplifypublishing.com

Library of Congress Control Number: 2026903721

CPSIA Code: PRV0326A

ISBN-13: 979-8-90026-078-5

Printed in the United States

This book is dedicated and a love letter to those seeking your true soul and your truest purpose. And to my great warrior father, Mike Breen. He has always been my guide and protector.

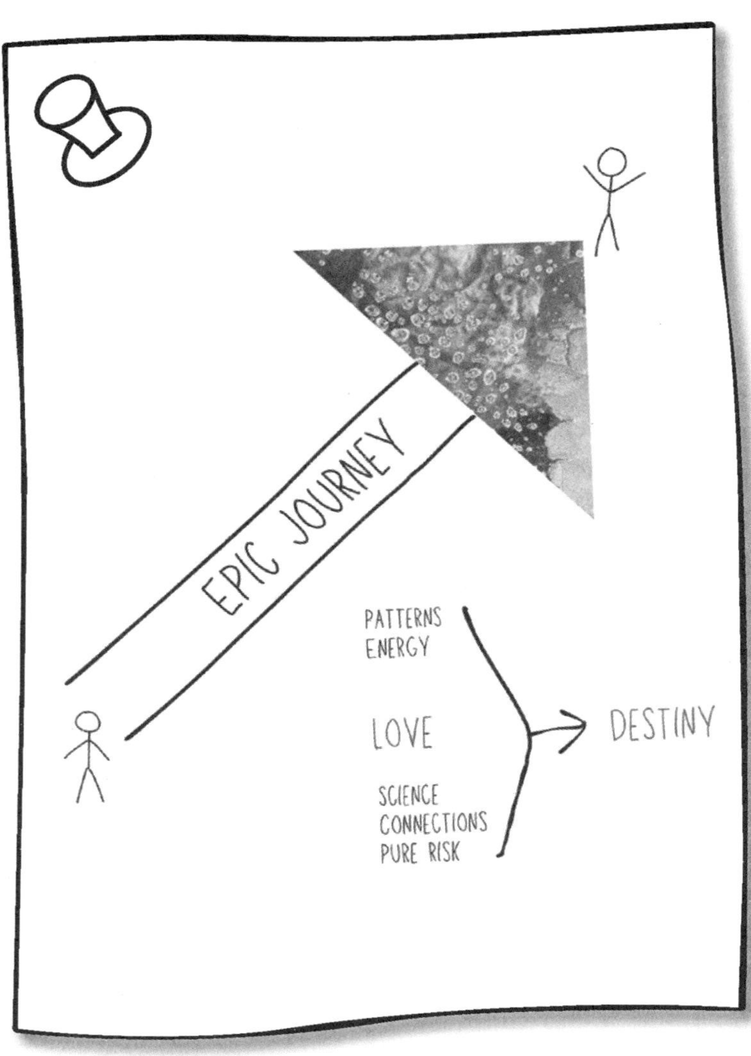
EPIC JOURNEY
PATTERNS
ENERGY
LOVE
SCIENCE
CONNECTIONS
PURE RISK
DESTINY

ACKNOWLEDGMENTS

THANK YOU to Nina Spahn, Jack Callahan, and your team at Amplify for taking the manuscript from its original form to publication.

And to my editorial team, including Maggie Hamilton, Leela Williams, Charlotte Humphrys, and Margie Tubbs, thank you for recommending my book to be included in the book club.

Also thank you to Ianthe Mauro for making my original drawings understandable for a mass audience. I am endlessly grateful for all the visionaries in my life who have shown the path to meaning, honor, bravery, and purpose.

INTRODUCTION

by Deepak Chopra, MD

SOME TIME BACK a number of colleagues spoke to me about a manuscript by Justin Breen at an AI well-being event, suggesting I might be interested in the manuscript, as it was based on the Seventh Spiritual Law of Success, the Law of Dharma.

This Law of Dharma teaches that each of us has a unique purpose, a divine calling encoded within our very being. We are not here by accident; we have come into this world to express our highest potential. At the deepest level, our journey begins with self-discovery—the realization that beyond our fleeting identities and conditioned roles, we are infinite, spiritual beings having a human experience. When we awaken to this truth, we align with the intelligence of the universe, allowing it to guide us toward our dharma.

Every soul is born with a unique talent, a gift so intrinsic that it flows effortlessly when we engage in it. This talent is not random; it is a sacred blueprint that, when honored, brings a sense of timeless joy. When we immerse ourselves in what we love, we tap into the creative field of infinite possibility. Time disappears, and we enter the realm of pure flow—this is the whisper of dharma calling us home.

Yet the highest expression of dharma is not just the pursuit of personal joy, but the act of using our gifts in service to others.

When we ask not "What can I get?" but "How can I serve?" we shift into a state of abundance. The universe supports those who contribute to the greater whole. In giving, we receive. In service, we expand. This is the secret of effortless success: When your dharma aligns with the needs of the world, prosperity and fulfillment naturally follow.

—Deepak

FOREWORD

ONE OF THE VERY FIRST BOOKS I reviewed this year was *Epic Journey*. I appreciated its central message of the Law of Dharma, or the Law of Purpose, a road map to guide the reader to higher levels of consciousness.

There are journeys and journeys in life. *Epic Journey* is for those who sense a boundlessness arising within, an ache to push beyond the familiar, beyond the well-worn grooves of life, to access something deeper, more nourishing, more profound.

An epic journey is at its most powerful when taken alone. It is a profound inner and outer journey, that can transform every part of us, and how first and foremost we choose to show up in the world.

Epic journeys are not for the fainthearted. They are designed to awaken the heroic self in us. One of the main reasons for including Justin's book in the book club was his desire to share his journey, to help inspire everyone to live up to their truest purpose, no matter what. He believes the outcome is worth it. Always.

We were drawn to this rich blend of love and connections, science and energy, patterns and pure risk—the very purest of pure risk being finding true love. *Epic Journey* is a book of heart.

—Maggie Hamilton

CONTENTS

HEED THE CALL

A JOURNEY OF EXQUISITE POSSIBILITIES lies before you, an invitation to embrace a new way of being in the world, and boundlessness is the key. Everyone is capable of being boundless. The boundless person understands that there are no beginnings and endings, and no start or finish line. They think of life as an endless pool of opportunities, instead of a race to the end.

Every single one of us has the ability to be boundless. Thinking outside the box doesn't resonate with boundless people, because they understand that there is no box to start with, and that we are infinite, immortal, and universal.

From this point on, when I speak of visionaries I'm referring to boundless individuals. I'm not referring to visionaries in the traditional sense, like an entrepreneur with a thousand ideas for the future of their company. I'm talking about people who see opportunities beyond the norms of society, and use their talents to help others to create good in the world.

These kinds of people are likely to follow the Law of Dharma, as laid out in Dr. Chopra's book *The Seven Spiritual Laws of Success*, which encourages people to find their life's purpose, then use that purpose, and their skills, to help others. The Law of Dharma says that we must look into our hearts to find our life's purpose, so that we can better serve humanity.

The heart is the center of our consciousness. Many people may not be aware that they are their own energy field. And most of our energy comes from this two-fist-sized organ called our heart—from the Latin word *cor*, which evolved to "courage." Having courage is all heart—literally.

Did you know that one human heart will complete about 100,000 beats per day, 35 million per year, and 2.5 billion over an average lifetime? That equates to one million barrels of blood, enough to fill a bunch of oil tankers. Blood passes through the body at about three feet per second, and goes through the entire body in about one minute.

Massive movement and energy are contained inside all of us. The heart, which began beating in utero before the brain even started to form, is so powerful that it creates its own electromagnetic field around the body, a magnetic field that extends in all directions, several feet away from the core. The heart contains cardiac ganglia, which the nonprofit HeartMath Institute describes as "little brains in the heart."

To simplify all this anatomy—the heart is at the center of everything within the body. The heart feeds the body with blood and feeds the brain, and its four hundred miles of capillaries, with essential information. Research now suggests that the heart-brain communicates more with the head-brain than the head-brain does with the heart-brain.

So, let me encourage you to become aware of what you feed

your heart. A study I came across required its participants to listen to several types of music. They were then tested to see how their autonomic nervous system and immune functions were affected. The results were startling. Many of those who listened to grunge rock measured higher rates of hostility, fatigue, sadness, and tension. In contrast, for most of those who listened to just fifteen minutes of "designer music," which is like a blend of jazz and soul (makes sense that it's soul music), their caring, mental clarity, relaxation, and vigor increased. I've now started listening to recorded meditations and videos from Dr. Joe Dispenza, one of the world's foremost leaders in meditation, to further connect my heart's power to my brain.

So how do we do all this? A great friend, Dr. Carlos Warter—a real-life version of the main character, Santiago, from Paulo Coelho's famous book, *The Alchemist*—has a simple way for people to listen to their heart. In his great book, *Who Do You Think You Are?*, Warter writes:

> Relax your solar plexus and stay relaxed. Then relax your belly. Concentrate the will that's there to say, "I am going to open my heart, **now.**" It [this heart connection] doesn't happen from the outside; it happens because you allow it, you will it, you determine it, you commit to it.

I have employed this exercise faithfully since discovering it recently. I say, *I am going to open my heart,* ***now*** multiple times a day, and sometimes out loud. It is calming. I can also feel the blood pumping in, otherwise ultimate silence and peace.

This is one of many patterns I use each day to slip into alignment, to a boundlessness framework. The favorite pattern or saying

I've used for some time is: *The right mindset attracts the right network and creates the right opportunities.* By incorporating the Law of Dharma, I have expanded my consciousness to realize that a pure heart attracts an abundant life. So, my mantra is now: *A grateful heart creates an abundant mindset that creates an exponential network which then creates limitless opportunities.*

Note, this pattern doesn't start with your mindset. It always begins with your **heart**.

To activate this mantra, I created a process, the Boundless Communication System (or BCS), for when I need to make a decision. How do I do this? It's about opening my heart, listening to it, then providing it with the best music and wisdom possible. So, when making a decision, I start by checking in with my heart to understand how I am **feeling** about a decision. This is the most important step. I ask myself: *How do I feel about what's happening?* After I have understood my emotions, the feelings move to my brain, where I think about my likely decision from all logical angles. Once I have understood a decision from the perspective of my heart and my brain, I can use my voice and put my decision into words. Then I use my hands and my body to put it into action.

Almost every decision I make now commences with how my heart is reacting. In the rare moments something feels 100 percent right in the heart, I go for it. 100 percent. Period. That's only happened a few times in my life, including the feeling I experienced to make me start writing this book. If there's something to question, which is the other 99 percent of the time, using the BCS process, I'll do a deep dive to see what's wrong, what needs tweaking, what needs to go.

Never doubt that your heart is a powerful organ. It can be your top decision-maker as well. Before you make a decision, see how you feel. Find somewhere quiet where you can listen to your

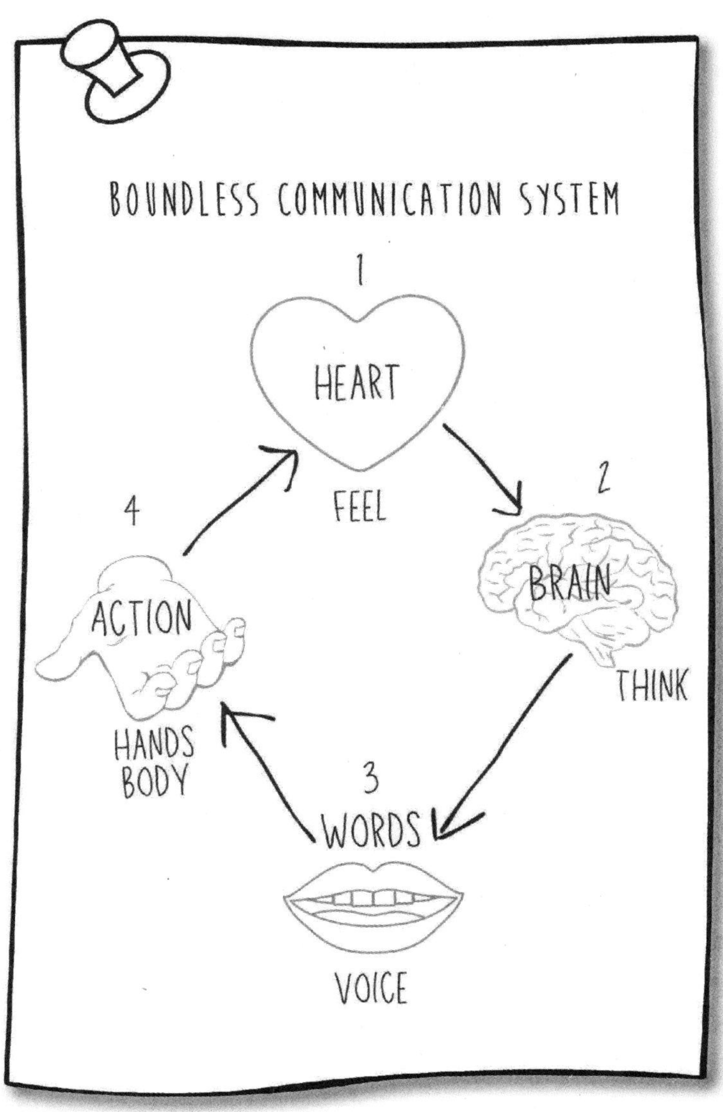
BOUNDLESS COMMUNICATION SYSTEM
1
HEART
FEEL
2
BRAIN
THINK
3
WORDS
VOICE
4
ACTION
HANDS
BODY

heart. As Proverbs 4:23 states: "Above all else, guard your heart, for everything you do flows from it." Awareness is key here, and as you start to tune into your heart on a regular basis, you'll become more aware of your body's true leader.

One quick example: I've always disliked the word "business." I've often questioned it, wondered why people cared so much about it, and was shocked by how business was saluted and trumpeted by the majority of society. My heart inspired me to look up the actual root of the word. It turns out it comes from the Old English word *bisignis* which literally means "anxiety." Or, as used in current English . . .

- *How's your "business" going? . . . How's your "anxiety" going?*
- *Let's 10x your "business!" . . . Let's 10x your "anxiety!"*
- *Hey, I know this great "business" coach. . . . Hey, I know this great "anxiety" coach.*
- *I'm majoring in "business." . . . I'm majoring in "anxiety."*

Another example is the phrase "pork-barreling," which now refers to questionable government spending that benefits individual members of Congress. Before this, in the early eighteenth century, it used to mean a literal barrel of pork. The pork was preserved in large wooden barrels, and the phrase "dipping into the pork barrel" became a common phrase that meant taking a share of money out of the household budget.

Over time, words change their meanings. Words, of course, are also energy. To many people, business means simply a career, an income, and success in the modern sense of the word. However, it's interesting to see where words come from, because words have a boundless quality. They change, adapt, and become boundless over millennia.

Yet regardless of the passage of time, your heart is the heart of all you seek. The living core of your life journey. Sometimes the journey has new beginnings. Though we have a great amount of trust in our heart functions, throughout your life this trust can start and stop and start again. A year ago, I had a conversation with Roosevelt Giles, who had undergone recent medical procedures to improve his heart function. He said, "When you go through something like this, you lose trust in your heart . . . not the physical but the mental [aspect of the heart]. You have to allow yourself time to trust your heart again, and that takes time." It took him twelve weeks. He continued, "God aligns people to be in your life at a certain time; like connective tissue . . . all things align the way they are supposed to."

So, even though we may lose trust in our heart's center (or as it's commonly referred to in Eastern philosophy, our "heart chakra") from time to time, it's essential we regain this, because everything starts with the heart center. It's the center of your relationships, your passions, your desires, your personality.

When fate steps in and causes us to distrust our heart center, this may be the perfect opportunity for a new beginning in our lives. Allowing ourselves to re-evaluate our heart's center, our desires, our relationships, and our hopes, can bring us new joys we might never have considered. This recalibration can set us on new journeys in our lives.

Let's face it, life is not a singular voyage. We undertake many journeys in a lifetime, because our lives are constantly evolving. Sometimes this can happen in an instant; sometimes this is a slow process. Regardless of the speed at which our hearts change, one thing is true: We are always changing. So, be open to the fact that your relationship with your heart may change over your lifetime, and let it happen.

While most hearts are the same size, differing very little from individual to individual, we often refer to certain people as having a "big heart." What I want you to realize is these people with big hearts actually have boundless hearts, no matter their physical size. It may differ in animals, but in humans, a big heart relates to someone's kindness. When it comes to animals, and in particular thoroughbreds, it literally means they have a big heart.

In my opinion, the greatest horse of all time, and I don't think his greatness will ever be surpassed, was the 1973 Triple Crown winner, Secretariat. *Sports Illustrated* reporter, Bill Nack, would sit outside Secretariat's stable for days on end just to observe him. I met Bill once before he passed away, at Churchill Downs in 1999, a week before the Kentucky Derby. At the time, I was an aspiring sports journalist. Bill was a kind man who helped me simplify some of my earliest articles. I always wanted to be a great journalist like him. He had a "Nack" for it, pun intended.

Nack wrote an article after Secretariat was put down and a necropsy performed on the horse. The professor who performed the necropsy, Dr. Thomas Swerczek, said that all of Secretariat's vital organs were normal size, except for his heart. The professor said that Secretariat's heart was double the average size, and a third larger than any horse heart he had ever seen before. I think about this story regularly. Maybe it was because it began with the final stoppage of an extraordinary heart inside the most extraordinary superhorse. Secretariat was born with a big heart, which he put to good use.

Boundless people are bighearted. They put their heart to good use. They constantly engage in activities that will help others. Like Bill who helped me, and from whom I learned so much, boundless individuals assist others. They willingly mentor them to achieve their goals and help them get what they want out of life.

Secretariat had the heart capacity to do things other horses couldn't. He used that uniquely massive heart to win the Triple Crown, including the Belmont Stakes, by a record thirty-one lengths. Boundless people do the same thing. They use their big hearts to go the extra mile for others; they lift them up, to set them on their way.

The importance of the heart goes beyond its importance in the physical body. The heart has been a symbol of love and kindness throughout history. The ancient Romans associated the heart with Venus, the goddess of love, who is said to have set hearts on fire with her child Cupid. In the Bible, Jesus's followers began to worship this great teacher, often captured in popular images with Jesus's glowing heart visible for all to see.

Throughout the ages, the heart has been associated with love, kindness, caring, and being magnanimous. Boundless people have all of these qualities. A boundless individual is not only a visionary. Like Secretariat, they have a good heart **and** they put it to good use.

EPIC TAKEAWAYS

- ✓ The heart is the center of it all. A grateful heart creates an abundant mindset, which then creates an exponential network from which limitless opportunities flow.
- ✓ Words, feelings, and interpretations are boundless.
- ✓ Step into a new relationship with your heart at different points in your life.
- ✓ Bighearted people make good use of their talents to help others.

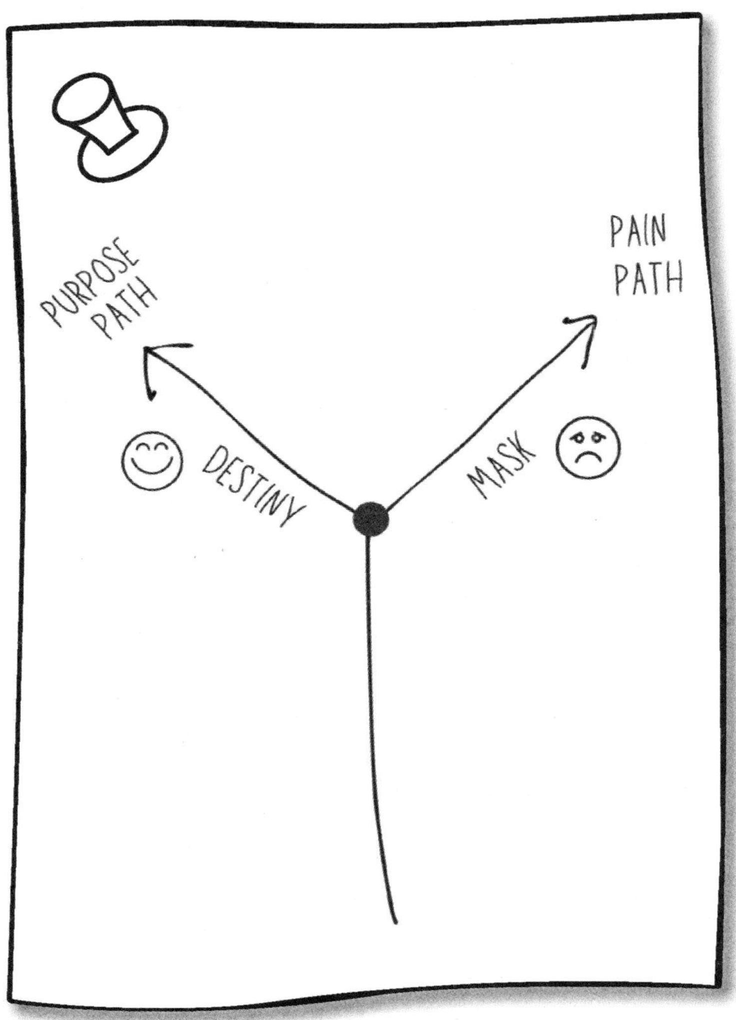
PURPOSE PATH
PAIN PATH
DESTINY
MASK

WHAT'S YOUR PURPOSE?

PURPOSE IS CENTRAL TO OUR JOURNEY, and who we choose to walk with on this journey is central too. To function at my optimal level and uncover my life purpose, I needed to understand which individuals were going to be an important part of my journey. Who was going to be there through thick and thin to help me? Who was destined to come and go? Put simply, for me to operate at my best, I needed to understand who my inner circle is, and who my acquaintances are (the interesting people I stumble across).

So, I created an index that categorizes people lovingly and caringly into four groups:

1. Who do you love?
2. Who do you like?
3. Who is interesting?
4. Who is important?

I encourage you to think about which people in your life fall into these categories. Do this caringly. For me, this file is priceless. I recommend you create your own priceless file. Once you understand who you love, it becomes easier to understand your purpose. As Viktor Frankl, author of *Man's Search for Meaning,* said, "The meaning of life is to give life meaning." We cannot be told our purpose. There is no universal meaning of life that encompasses all individuals, all desires, and all passions. We must search for our **own** meaning by understanding who we truly love, then from the depth of this love, life's purpose flows.

As a journalist, I regularly asked people who they love and what their purpose was. As a PR firm owner, same thing. Running a global connectivity platform and connecting with the world's leading entrepreneurs all day, five days a week, I hone in on their passions, their purpose. I recommend that you also contemplate these questions. Ask yourself what or who you love the most. In my case, my loved ones are directly related to my life's purpose and meaning. When you find out what or who you love, your life purpose becomes clear. Of course, after being the best father I can be to my children, the best partner I can be to my wife, the best son, brother, nephew, and best friend, my wider purpose is in connecting individuals to serve humanity.

There are certain discussions and thoughts that you can share with the ones you love, rather than those you like or find interesting. The ones you love, and who love you, are without judgment, without fear, and without misinterpretation. A loved one and I were talking about how triangles are the strongest shape. It's no surprise then that bridges are made out of them, because triangles are inherently rigid. We also see connections, relationships, and partnerships as triangles.

As we then move on to contemplate our passions, we become aware of what we're up against. We see that the biggest issue the world faces is that the overwhelming majority of capital—especially in the venture capital space—is controlled by egotistical men, "suns" shining brightly through their own powerful egos. These individuals melt most things in their way, not caring what they torch, burn, or eviscerate. It's all about serving their own light.

How can we change this? The balance comes from combining these "Father Suns" with "Mother Earths." We'll look at this in more detail later, but basically, neutral "moons" can be Father Suns at times and Mother Earths during others. This then forms the triangle structure like a universal, cosmic work of geometrical art. A beautiful bridge.

My great friend Jennifer Hill, who is truly boundless and one of the best connectors ever, went further to create the "Golden Triangle." She describes this as "creating greater coherence between ourselves, our loved ones, and our purpose." These three pillars are deeply interconnected and, when combined, reveal to us what our individual meaning of life is.

Let me explain. In our company, I am the Father Sun who had the original light idea. But that's where my contribution stops. If I were involved in the day-to-day detail, I'd wipe out the company, like Mount Vesuvius did to Pompeii and Herculaneum on August 24, 79 AD.

My wife tries hard to keep me grounded within the family and the company. Our company members have their own skill sets, ranging from empathy to competition and everything in between. With every partnership and connection that we make, I insist there are three collaborators, with at least one who serves as Mother Earth. This doesn't necessarily need to be an actual woman, but it has to be someone with more feminine energy. That way, the traditional masculine ego is mitigated and channeled properly. I've found that each of the collaborators is living in their own Golden

Triangle, unlocking consciousness within themselves, their loved ones, and their purpose.

If we want our collaborations to be successful, we need to have a Father Sun, a Neutral Moon, and a Mother Earth to achieve a productive balance. I encourage you to do the same. Within your loved ones, identify the people who fit into these three categories. Once you create your own dynamic trio, you will be able to have meaningful conversations, to understand yourself and your philosophies at a deeper level.

In my own discussions with loved ones, I have found what is needed to collaborate with others. But for these conversations to be effective, you must have them with loved ones, not with acquaintances. Only then can you plumb the depth you seek.

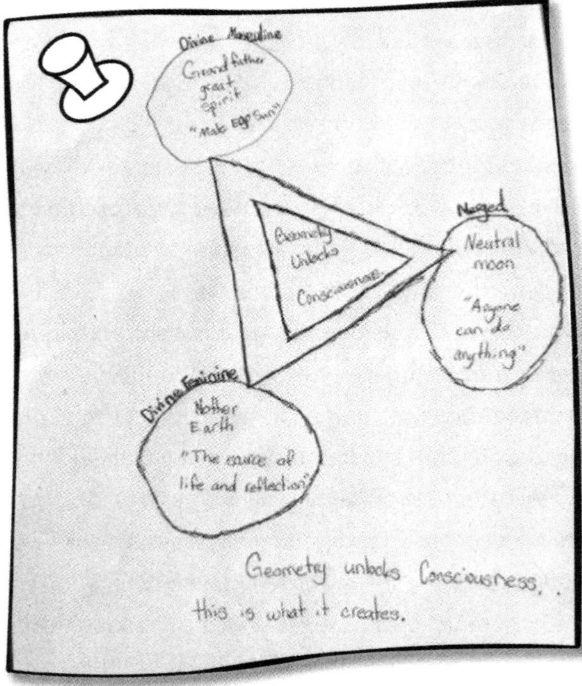

Like Clark Kent, I'm also a reporter. Clark had individuals he truly loved: his parents, Lois, Jimmy Olsen, and Perry White. Together, they helped create and hold his greater purpose. *Truth, justice, and a better tomorrow* is modern-day Superman's motto. It's also the creed of visionaries and boundless people. I connect with fresh thinkers from all over the world, and what I've observed is that boundless individuals do, from time to time, risk their liberties. They make very few excuses and see the challenges that come their way as opportunities.

Another of my life's purposes is to help individuals break out of their prison. Have you ever met, read about, or seen movies about multi-millionaires who are in their own heart and mind prisons? Searching for meaning, happiness, power, status, or something else, they haven't yet figured out why they still feel unfulfilled. These characters in movies or books often have an endless drive for more, which leaves less and less within the soul. Think of Frank Abagnale Jr. from the movie *Catch Me If You Can*, or Jordan Belfort from *The Wolf of Wall Street*, who were never satisfied with the huge amounts of money they made, who always felt like they needed more.

Once you give an individual a purpose,
they can strive for greater things.
Once you give someone a destination,
they know how to begin a journey.

Then there are actual prisons, and lots of movies, such as *The Longest Yard*, about prisons. Like Burt Reynolds, I also visited correctional institutions to play sport with the inmates. After just a few hours behind steel gates and twenty-foot-high cement walls covered with barbed wire, surrounded by the players, I could feel the hopelessness within that space. However, given the opportunity to play a game, I witnessed an immediate competitiveness among inmates—the will to win, to achieve, to find purpose, if only to win one lousy match.

Once you give an individual a purpose, they can strive for greater things. Once you give someone a destination, they know how to begin a journey.

Millionaires have the same intensity as prisoners behind the small glass opening of solitary confinement. That's passion all right. The question is, what do we intend to do with our passion? Do we plan to use it for selfish or destructive purposes, or for good? And what happens to that passion when life takes you down?

No doubt we're all familiar with Bob Dylan's song, *Hurricane*, about an individual who was wrongly imprisoned. I encountered Alphonso James, who was in a Wisconsin prison for more than three decades after being wrongly convicted of first-degree murder in the mid-1980s. Alphonso was finally paroled on Valentine's Day 2017, after further evidence proved he wasn't even at the scene.

How James lives, feels, and thinks, even after such a great injustice, is cleansing. I so love his favorite quote: "He that is Perfect is perfecting perfection in me." Explaining why this was his favorite quote, James said, "Throughout the years this came to mean different things. However, the overall impact this had on me is I gain a sense of Balance. My mind, soul, and spirit had to align with my purpose."

James's favorite quote mirrors one of my own favorites from the late, great Earl Nightingale: "Success is the progressive realization of a worthy ideal." This also aligns with the first thing I do every single day, which is uttering the Prayer of Jabez from the Bible: "Oh, that You would bless me indeed, and enlarge my territory, that Your hand would be with me, and that You would keep me from evil."

To bring all these powerful quotes into simple, actionable steps, I focus each day on a higher power guiding my purpose, praying for that higher power to guide me in the best, most positive way, so that I can stay purely focused on my purpose of connecting visionaries to serve humanity.

Let me be clear, I am not what one would describe as a religious person, but I strongly believe and trust in a higher power and like to learn from the richness of other faiths, as there is always more wisdom to absorb.

The Quran says it takes forty years for someone to reach maturity. Moses and his followers spent forty years in the desert after leaving Egypt. In my experience, it takes a long time to truly embrace enough life experiences and teachings, to learn what matters in life. My quest always is to find that pure "worthy ideal." To achieve this, I like to talk to many people in their sixties, seventies, and eighties, who haven't yet found that ideal and are still searching. And, because they're serious about their search, I have no doubt that they will find what they're looking for.

James's story and his quote about *perfecting perfection in me* is a wonderful start for us all. It allowed this man, who could so easily have ended up broken and bitter, to gain balance, to align his mind, soul, and spirit with a deep purpose. Balance and purpose are everything. They free up our mind, body, and soul from whatever internal prison we find ourselves in. They open the door into external abundance, which reaches every part of our being.

Of course, all these possibilities bring us back to heart. Imagine the power of the human mind when combined with an enormous, magnanimous heart. Nelson Mandela was the personification of this. He, at all times, understood that his purpose in life was to permanently change the country he was born in, and to bring freedom to all who lived in South Africa. His heart was so huge that he constantly forgave those who had imprisoned him. As Mandela said, "A good head and a good heart are always a formidable combination." Mandela stood out as an individual who combined his heart and mind to create a profound sense of purpose for the good of his loved ones and for humanity itself.

The Law of Dharma reminds us that we all have **unique** talents and purposes, and that we should ask ourselves how we can use these skills to serve others. To better serve the planet, understand what and whom we love, and through this knowledge realize our purpose. By then shifting our passions from focusing on our hearts to our minds, we can better unpack our purpose, then use all the intelligence we have to put it to good use, by helping others.

EPIC TAKEAWAYS

- ✓ Find out who you love, as this will lead you to your purpose.
- ✓ Collaborate with loved ones to ensure you have the benefit of different points of view.
- ✓ To discover your true purpose, you must be able to combine your heart's desire and critical thinking.

THE BOUNDLESS JOURNEY

AS WE CONTEMPLATE a heart-centered journey ahead, informed by all the wisdom we can gather, it's important to note that this is the path of boundlessness, of expansive actions, of limitless thinking. Every journey, however, starts with the first step. As American tennis player Arthur Ashe famously said, "Success is a journey, not a destination." I believe a great place to start a journey is to find out who got you here, so that you can better understand yourself, and the legacy that you have been born into.

In the words of Oscar Wilde: "To love oneself is the beginning of a lifelong romance." So, let the romance begin!

I researched my heritage as far back as I could, learning my father's parents gambled everything, and came to this country speaking no English. These are important details. They help us sense the energies we're emerging from. I also learned I'm named in honor of my grandmother, Ida, who arrived in the US in the late 1800s. She worked sixty to seventy hours a week at Marshall Field for $3 a week, an improvement from her previous employment.

Around 1910, Ida married my grandfather, a tailor/entrepreneur/heavy Schnapps drinker named Nathan. The couple had four boys and lived in a small apartment in the northwestern Chicago suburb of Elgin, Illinois. I only know all of this because one of their children, the youngest named Harold (though everyone called him Beaver) wrote a detailed history of the family in 1979. The coolest part is that football legend Red Grange was our family's ice deliveryman, while he was on his way to becoming a superstar at the University of Illinois. Everyone called my grandmother "Shorty," because she was less than five feet tall and played shortstop during stickball games with her four sons.

From my Uncle Beaver's family history:

> An interesting story Shorty used to tell was that the iceman during that summer was a friendly, playful, young redheaded University of Illinois student, who would always stop and play with the four little Breen boys. To Shorty's perpetual consternation, "Red" would roughhouse with them, throwing them into the air and catching them to the boys' great delight and Shorty's constant fear. Finally, she would give him hell and chase him off, but he was always back the next day.

All four Breen boys, including my dad Mike, risked death to serve proudly in World War II. It's a miracle all four survived, went to college, then had their own families. They and my grandparents were featured in many national articles in the early 1940s, because it was rare to send all four children to war. Think *Saving Private Ryan*, but where all made it through the endless battles. Uncle Beaver was declared dead after a plane crash in England. Luckily, the Army got it wrong. He was maimed and covered in burns, but survived and was featured in an article about his not being dead. His son, Aaron, would eventually share that article in a book about my dad's family titled *Assess. Adjust. Adapt . . . A Strategy for Perseverance Used by Three Generations of Breens in America.*

I found an article titled *Four Sons in the Army* about my father's family from the May 8, 1942, edition of the *Chicago Jewish Chronicle.* Its final paragraphs describe the true gift of my grandmother:

> I scanned the shelves of books, the copy-crammed notebooks and records of court cases kept by the lawyer-son (my dad) for the past two years—objects upon which the mother looks with tear-dimmed eyes in her moments of loneliness, and which soothe her solitude. I looked at all these things which to me seemed to transform this humble kitchen into a museum of motherlove and sacrifice—an environment from which came forth, under the most adverse circumstances of want and privation, four gifted sons who have given their parents more cause for pride than the sons of the wealthiest mansions could have done.
>
> This small, frail old mother suddenly loomed in my eyes like a titan, a true soldier who on the battlefield of a gray life, has won the battle on behalf of her boys, and who is now sending them forth to help win the mighty conflict, which is to decide the destiny of the nation and world. And as I felt her warm and trembling hand in mine when we parted, I was seized by an impulse to salute her as my superior, and to say, "Goodbye, Colonel!"

Every time I see these words I feel her power and cannot help but cry and salute her.

My father personally lived through the Spanish Flu, World Wars I and II, the Great Depression, and the Cold War, and he served in Korea and "worked" with leaders like Jimmy Hoffa, former president of the International Brotherhood of Teamsters. I was told he cried only one time as an adult, when his mom was dying and he had to drive her to a nursing home. My dad took care of my grandmother and lived with her for decades after my grandfather died, after World War II in the mid-1940s.

My dad's best friend was killed in a famous gangland mafia hit in 1983. If you watch the movies *Casino* and *The Irishman,* you can learn about and/or watch the killing. One of my first memories was my dad trying to hide our family, because he thought he, and possibly his wife and children, would be assassinated next. He did not cry during those moments.

My dad was always the "clean man" in an operation. Even when he was younger, he was involved in that world. As Uncle Beaver explained:

> Mike graduated from high school in 1934 and, during his grade school and high school years, was an inveterate reader, who made great use of the Elgin Public Library. Mike's main hobby was sports, especially basketball and baseball, besides his reading. Upon graduation from high school, Jack Heslin [a local gangster] and some of Jack's close friends—Bob Kemler, a lawyer; brother Bill, a businessman; and Jack Schmidt, part-owner of the cooperage factory—decided that all four would chip in and send Mike to school so he could become a lawyer.

> Actually, Jack Heslin just told the other three what he, Jack Heslin, had decided. Jack was generous and benevolent, but was not above looking to some potential future return from Mike as one of his "future lawyers." Adding together whatever money the family could supply, the part-time job earnings, and savings from Mike's and Jack Heslin's "syndicate" contribution, Mike was able to go to a Jesuit School in Dubuque, Iowa, called Columbia College [later renamed Loras College]. Mike took his two years of pre-law there, then applied and was accepted into DePaul Law School in Chicago. He commuted into Chicago daily for three years. On Saturdays and other days off, he worked in Chicago selling shoes.

My mom endured a horrific childhood of abuse and poverty. Her father abandoned the family when she was a young child, and her mother, the only biological grandparent I ever met, suffered from extreme mental illness. When the bill collectors came to her home, my grandmother would lock herself in a room and hide . . . waiting and waiting for them to stop banging on the front door or looking through the windows. She was kind to me, but chain-smoked whenever I visited her, while we watched *Jeopardy!* or some other game show. The last time I saw her she had experienced a stroke and could barely move, but still tried to climb a staircase on her hands and knees. She made it to the top. Determination. No excuses.

My mother has always protected her sisters and brother, while supporting all of my siblings. She's the purest survivor of anyone I've ever met, and all I do is talk to survivors. She's also one of the best connectors I've ever seen. She envisions things well before most humans, like a seer.

I talk to my dad quite a bit, especially when I visit his graveside. My father, Mike, was sixty-one when I was born, and my mother, Bonni, was twenty-seven. They met after a drunk driver hit my father's car head-on, when my dad was in his late fifties. The drunk driver was killed instantly. My dad broke numerous bones and thought he was dead when he woke up and that my mom was his guiding angel.

My mom was actually his nurse. She—and everyone else—wanted him to date her mom, who was around the same age. But my dad was like me—he didn't care what anyone else thought. He followed his heart and intuition, no matter what. He put everything on the line because his gut told him to, and then his brilliant brain found a way to do it. No excuses.

I was born a few years later, followed by two younger brothers. Sadly, my youngest brother is no longer with us, due to a drug overdose when he was twenty-nine.

My father was a hero in World War II, as a First Lieutenant in the Battle of Hürtgen Forest in Germany and Belgium. He was shot down numerous times in combat on bombing missions. Many times, he wasn't wearing a parachute. He would just get back into another plane.

So, genetically, then connected through storytelling, I come from a line of visionaries seeking liberty. Forbears who would do whatever it takes to achieve that freedom. Then they wrote about how they achieved it. Everyone has these types of stories in their background, some more colorful, some less. The point is, it's important to know what stock you come from, to understand your heritage and your background, so you can appreciate how wonderful and enormous the efforts were to get you right here.

Be grateful for the opportunity to continue their legacy and create your legacy for the next generation. When you come from a place of appreciation and gratitude for being here, go back into your heritage and make notes of the characteristics, habits, and beliefs that you inherited from your predecessors. How can you expand on those traits? If you had an uncle who was determined, how much more determined can you be? If you had a family member who was a trailblazer, what can you do to continue on their path?

Look at your life as a relay race with these individuals passing on the baton to you. The race is not complete. There are a lot of batons being passed on. So, find out what you can do to give your gifts to the next generation. As novelist Catherine Ryan Hyde said, "If you can't pay it back, pay it forward." Don't repay your parents and grandparents; pay it forward to the future generations who will benefit from it the most.

It's not just our blood relatives who influence our lives and shape our journeys. We regularly meet new people who set us on new paths, who come into our lives to teach us life lessons we otherwise might not experience. Twenty-five years ago, fresh out of college, I told The Crab Man I wanted to write a story about him and his great restaurant. The Crab Man was Bob Chinn, who died in 2022 after a ninety-nine-year life journey of serial entrepreneurship and service to his country. Mr. Chinn dropped out of high school to join the Army and eventually served in World War II—in Northern Ireland of all places. He never went back to school after the military. Instead, he became one of America's greatest restauranteurs. A quarter of a century ago, he also provided me with one of the most important lessons I've ever had.

Mr. Chinn's most well-known accomplishment was opening Bob Chinn's Crab House in 1982, when he was fifty-nine years old. Crab House would become one of this country's top-grossing restaurants. It started because a man, who dropped out of high school to serve his country with honor, decided to never stop fighting the battle of life.

He fought the battle of life despite launching numerous other restaurants that went bottom up, and the fact that Bob would drive to Chicago O'Hare International Airport to pick up fresh fish from Alaska and Hawaii well before sunrise. When he opened Crab House, he was fifty-nine years old—the age when most are thinking about phoning it in through retirement, and just three years before Americans can start collecting social security.

My family, led by my great warrior father, Mike, were among the first customers at Bob Chinn's Crab House. Back then, snow crab legs were about $9 a pound at the restaurant, which started at 250 seats and eventually expanded to 700. The Crab House served 2,500 meals a day, made up of 3,000 pounds of fresh seafood flown in from around the world. As the restaurant grew, Mr. Chinn stopped driving the delivery truck and instead parked a flashy Corvette in his special parking spot just outside the employee entrance.

Like Mr. Chinn, my father served in World War II. Unlike Mr. Chinn, my father survived endlessly brutal combat missions in Germany, Belgium, and other front-line locales. Dad was 61 years old when I was born and would be 108 if he were still alive. My father and Bob were friends. They hung out at Arlington Park horse track, and Mr. Chinn invited my family into his private box from time to time. The Crab House is one of the few places where a few people still remember my father, a great man with a brilliant brain and an even bigger heart, but our journey together will change that. It is an honor to be given a gift that somehow makes endless dendritic connections and, hopefully, will create massive, universal change. Those connections allow my dad to live for much longer, hopefully for many generations yet.

When I talked to Bob Chinn in 1999 about writing a story about him and Crab House, he provided one quote that I remember with much power and passion. Finally, twenty-five years later, I get to use it now. He said, "It would be a **disservice** to people to not tell them about this restaurant. They need to know that it exists."

Now a father of two warrior boys who love eating crab legs (about $59–$99 a pound now), lobster tails, and fresh fish at Bob Chinn's Crab House, I see what that seafood restaurant really is. It is Bob Chinn's gift to the world. It would be wrong of me not to tell people about it because he put all of himself—everything—into making it transcendent, special beyond special. It remains that way, even after his death.

It is the responsibility of all of us to share our gifts with the world. True gifts should not be kept secret, even if it does not come naturally to share those secret gifts. Like any great gift, my talents come from a higher power. This journey honors that higher power and the women and men, like my father and Bob Chinn, who will never stop fighting to share their gifts.

There are important people in your life who have a profound effect on you and mold the way you think. Sometimes, you'll want to pass that experience on to your children. The point of looking at your ancestry is that you can be very honest with yourself about your strengths and your shortcomings, those patterns that do and don't help you. I learned a lot from my father about being determined, how to keep fighting without any excuses, and how to fight for what I want. What family characteristics do you want to hold on to? What family traits do you wish to eliminate? Everyone has a black sheep in the family. You should be honest with yourself and find the traits you want to keep and the traits you want to remove.

After you have examined your heritage, ask yourself who you have brought into your life that you love. How can they help you to improve yourself? What do they bring to you? What lessons can you learn from them? What characteristics do they have that you don't? How do they balance you or empower you? How do they make you a better person? Look for these individuals in your life and see what they bring to make you more complete.

I implore you to look around and not try to do it all yourself. Everyone has friends, acquaintances, and loved ones with attributes that they don't have, that complement them. My partner brought that to the table. So, look for people who have complementing traits. If you're an accountant, find a salesperson. If you're a writer, find an editor. If you're a chef, find a waiter.

Take notice of individuals that come into your life. It's important to understand the categories they can take up with ease, and how to maximize the impact they have in your life. It's also important to understand how to maximize, to enhance **their** lives, because you have touched them. Part of being boundless and infinite is to appreciate everyone who comes into your life, no matter how momentary, and ensure that you touch people's lives in a way that empowers them.

EPIC TAKEAWAYS

- ✓ Begin with the greatest love of all—self-love. Improve on your family traits and dispense with those that don't resonate with you anymore.
- ✓ Find out where you came from and who you are, so you can understand where you're going and how you can pay it forward.
- ✓ Find people that balance you out with traits you may be missing.
- ✓ Touch other people's lives.

4 A NEW WAY OF OPERATING

HOW MUCH HAS THE PLUS (+) sign changed since its inception? These days we don't think twice before we dial internationally; we go straight to the + sign and the country code. In the classroom, the + sign is the symbol of addition. The + sign began with Latin (seems like everything originated with Latin) in the mid-1300s. The + sign was used as shorthand for the Latin word *et* which means "and." After more than one hundred years of nonexistence, the + sign re-emerged in Germany in the late 1400s in a publication, *Mercantile Arithmetic,* to indicate a surplus in business. The word "plus" itself is a Latin word meaning "more."

But enough of history. When I'm looking for entertainment, I go to my favorite streaming services like Disney+ or Paramount+ to give me a heightened experience. So, I'll leave you with the fact that + is very positive. Add a + to your name the next time you sign off an email or a text message, to remind yourself that you are boundless and endlessly positive.

The origin of number two is even more interesting. It's the smallest, and the only even, prime number. It dates back to Arabic Indic Brahmic script in the third century, when the number was written as two horizontal lines, like an = sign. By the way, the number two descends from Old English's *twā* (feminine) and *twēgen* (masculine).

Let's put all this together and examine the power of +2 relationships, souls, groups, and ways of feeling and thinking. From its origins, +2 could be written += or "more feminine/masculine." It is numerological perfection! Mark Fujiwara, the former cofounder of my second company, created a "+2 code" for identifying valued people, collaborators, and relationships. He lives by it.

Mark had talked about +2s so many times in our meetings that one of our members, Randy Molland, decided to double down and create a "+2 framework" cheat sheet that's brilliant for use at the highest level. He likes to use the +2 framework with his employees—current and future. He also uses it with his friends, family, and collaborators, and, of course, he uses it on himself.

In short, Randy identified five qualities that are needed to have a +2 relationship. Let's go through them one at a time.

The first quality is **listening more than speaking**. This notion goes back to ancient Greece, when Zeno, the founder of a school of philosophy called Stoicism, said, "We have two ears and one mouth, therefore we should listen twice as much as we speak." Listening more than speaking allows us to expand our knowledge and keep ourselves open-minded when meeting and connecting with others. The purpose of Stoicism is to become wise and therefore have a good life that serves an ethical goal. According to Stoicism, if we keep our mindset focused on gaining new knowledge, we will be able to lead better lives and serve a higher purpose.

So, keep yourself open and try to absorb as much information as you can when you are collaborating, rather than dominating the conversation with your take on things. That's not to say you shouldn't share your opinions and ideas when collaborating with others, only that it is essential to balance this with active listening and keeping a mindset that encourages learning.

The second quality of Randy's +2 framework is **having a giving mentality**, without expecting anything in return. A boundless person, as we have discussed, finds their unique skills in life and their purpose and puts their talents to good use by helping others. A boundless individual does not expect to receive anything in return, whether monetary gain or otherwise.

A visionary uses their skills to help others because they genuinely hope to improve the lives of those around them and to better society. It is not uncommon for a boundless person to experience monetary gain in return for their services, but this cannot be the driving factor behind a visionary's purpose. My great friend, Lee Benson, didn't know his biological father and was kicked out of home when he was a teenager. He grew up somehow doing the right things within a criminal and murderous family and started his first company $600,000 in debt. He then owned and led Able Aerospace before selling it for nine figures. He now spends his time helping senior leadership teams earn similar exits and has a massive music studio in his twelve-thousand-square-foot house for guests, where he plays a mean guitar.

Lee, who is in his sixties, has never married, and doesn't have children, shared that he wants to find the right person to leave his wealth to and share his life. After he said that, he released the most calming, beautiful exhalation of breath I've ever heard. It was pure peace. I wouldn't be surprised if Lee ends up like my dad, having kids in his sixties. While Lee certainly reaps the benefits of his labor and lives a more than comfortable life, he is still searching for ways to give. He wants to share his wealth with others and provide for those who need help, because he's always searching for a way to give.

A boundless person remains in a giving mentality and stays focused on how they can provide for others and better serve humanity. To ensure that I stay focused on a giving mentality, I must align myself with the hours of the day I am most productive.

This brings me to the third quality in the +2 framework, which is **having high character and alignment**. For me to produce the best work that will help the most people, I need to have a clear understanding of my circadian rhythm, to ensure that I have aligned my working hours of the day with my most productive ones. I prefer to work late at night. I know they say that the early bird gets the worm, but they're welcome to all the worms they want. I work better during the night.

I strongly suggest that everyone look into their own circadian rhythms and explore which time is best for them. Ask yourself: Are you a night owl? Are you an early riser? What is your optimal time? For me, the middle of the night is when I fully step into my flow. The feeling of being so consumed by an idea that sleep can't possibly stop me is beautiful. I love it. The solitude of the night, the darkness, and the quiet allow my mind to open up and be consumed by the thoughts swirling around in my head. I've done some great work in the middle of the night.

It was 2:17 a.m. when I wrote this. It was perfect for me. I looked outside, and my house was the only one with a light on. I'm sure some of you can resonate with this. Many of you reading this will be early to rest and early to rise individuals. So, I implore you to find your own rhythm. Pick a time when you are alone and have space to download everything you've taken in during the day. Some people check their inboxes and answer emails late at night, because that's the best time for them. I'm describing myself here. In the night, I'm completely alone with myself and have time to process the wave of information that has been thrown at me during the day.

My kind of visionaries are like night owls. They work best in the darkness and see their dream from every angle. Beyond that, I think that boundless people base their dreams on creating good in the world. Not just for themselves, but for others. So, while the solitude of working at night opens up my flow, I want to share my ideas with others so they can use them in their most productive hours, whenever they may be. For me, the universe speaks the loudest at night, away from the distractions and chaos of the day. I choose to listen to the universe when it's quietest. I don't expect the universe to shout at me to get my attention during the busyness of the day.

If you're wondering why the universe doesn't seem to be reaching out to you, speaking to you, or offering you the advice you are craving, perhaps you should choose the quietest hours of the day when no one else is around to welcome the universe in. I truly don't expect the universe to speak to me when I'm busy with work, chores, or my family. I listen to the universe in the quietest hours of the night. The universe is always sending you information, looking after you. Perhaps the universe doesn't feel like screaming it out above the noise. Perhaps it wants to quietly whisper its wisdom and inspiration to you when you can focus on it.

The universe is available to everyone. We are all boundless in one form or another. All we need to do is listen and we will be rewarded. We must decide what our vision is for our future, for the ones we love, and for our highest evolution. But first, we must search for the most suitable time that the universe wishes to communicate with us. We must find the most productive hours of the day, so that we can truly listen to the insights it gives us and implement them. It doesn't matter which hours work best for you; it's just a matter of ensuring we are aligned with our natural bodily rhythms.

The fourth component of the +2 framework is **prioritizing impact over income**. A boundless person is not focused on what they will gain from helping others. They simply hope to help as many people as they can. Knowing the right way to create a positive impact on as many people as possible is an essential skill set for a boundless person hoping to have positive effect on the world.

Most people know the story of Paul Revere and how he rode on horseback on April 18, 1775, warning Americans that the "British are coming! The British are coming!" and that the Revolutionary War was about to begin. What some might not know is that Revere was not the only person riding across America to issue this warning. William Dawes also set off from Boston on horseback at the same time as Revere—Revere north and Dawes south.

An article in *Harvard Business Review* explained why Dawes was lesser known than Revere. According to the 2005 *HBR* article "How to Build Your Network," both men had similar social standings and education; however Revere knew how to cultivate the right social network to create the highest impact for his goal. The article said that Revere was an "information broker" who was able to connect with different groups of people. He knew which people to convey his message to. He knew how to contact other "well-connected people" on his ride across America, and because of this, his message was spread effectively. By comparison, Dawes did not know who to contact to share his message with the greatest number of people, and as a result, his message was shared with far fewer people.

Revere was captured. Dawes escaped. Numerous articles, including those on History.com noted that Dawes's journey was far more daring, but that didn't matter because he didn't have the right PR. Paul Revere did. To me, Revere's name and his serving as an "information broker" symbolizes the real meaning of the term PR. He had the optimal network of valued alliances. People he could trust. People who could trust him. Leaders with their own networks of trusted connections. The word spread and continued well after both men died. Put simply, Paul Revere was information brokering during his ride to glory and is remembered because he knew the right leaders, such as John Hancock and Samuel Adams. He had the right connections and optimally brokered the information he had available.

Like Revere, a visionary is focused on ensuring that their impact is widespread, with minimal focus on the money they may stand to gain from their venture. So, when you are approaching a new venture, think about the types of people you will need to connect with to ensure that your project has the most impact—the most positive impact on those it will affect. A boundless person is always focused on how to best help others, rather than making money.

This brings me to the fifth and final quality of the +2 framework, which is to constantly **ask the question "How can I help you?"** Dr. Wayne Dyer, described by many as the father of inspiration, has offered countless innovative insights. The one that stuck most firmly with me was that for us to find our purpose and be fulfilled, we must find a way to serve humanity. He encouraged us to ask the question "How may I serve?" According to Dr. Dyer, by keeping service at the forefront of our mentality, we can lead fulfilled lives and feel secure in our purpose in life. In his words:

> The greatest joy comes from giving and serving. That's much better than the discomfort and distress of focusing exclusively on yourself and what's in it for you. When you make the shift to supporting others in your life, without expecting anything in return, you'll think less about what you want, and find comfort and joy in the act of giving and serving. This giving, loving, serving person is the real you.

This concept is essential to ensure that the focus on any boundless person's venture stays centered on helping others, rather than on personal gain. When we stay focused on serving and helping others, our lives will feel fulfilled. This "serving" mentality is perhaps the most essential of all the components in the +2 framework, because it ensures that the basis of a relationship or collaboration is always about the positive effect it will have on humanity.

By using the +2 framework, you will be able to find quality working relationships that prioritize the improvement of society and cultivate relationships that are constantly evolving and expanding. So, I encourage you to use the +2 framework when selecting people to work with you on your future endeavors. Also, use it as a checklist for yourself of all the qualities that ensure a growth mindset, to keep yourself in the zone of helping others.

+2
SOUL INTERACTION
+
=
+=
=
+

EPIC TAKEAWAYS

- ✓ Listen more than you speak.
- ✓ Have a giving mentality without expecting anything in return.
- ✓ Ensure that your circadian rhythm is aligned to have high character.
- ✓ Prioritize impact over income.
- ✓ Ask, "How can I help you?"

NOTE THE MUSIC

LIFE'S COMPLICATED AND CHALLENGING AT TIMES, but I'm here to tell you, it can also be exhilarating and full of promise. So, how can you live a full life, one that enables you to reach your fullest potential? We're each on a journey, a different journey. Maybe you're looking for answers. Maybe you're looking for meaning. Perhaps you're looking for your soulmate, a best friend, a partner or guide, a mentor or new family, or that one perfect person who completely understands you.

I'm in search of music. What do I mean by this? I'm on the lookout for people, places, and experiences that deliver pure harmony. How do I do this? I pay attention to notes, the rhythm that others give off. I pay attention to their beat—all in search of the perfect beat, the perfect pattern to perfect all I seek to do. And, I suggest some part of you is also in search of music. Why? Because music is love.

Music provides us with sequence and connectivity. It offers a life of great highs and lows, and differing pitches. Music is a direct pathway to the heart, a profound journey through emotion and feeling, joy and sorrow, life and death, and into the beyond.

Charlie Parker, one of the greatest jazz musicians ever, said, "Music is your own experience, your thoughts, your wisdom." Put simply, it's how you show up in the world. So, if you want to change your life, to take it up a peg or two, or more, then you need to pay attention to your notes. How are you sounding right now? What thoughts, what insights do you ache to sound, and then share with the world? How is your music best expressed? Where is it you most want it to take you? What is the sound of the place you yearn to be?

Music gives a soul to the Universe, wings to the mind, flight to the imagination, and life to everything.

Plato, ancient Greek philosopher

If we want to live differently, then we need to make some changes. How do we do this? We need to get clear about what we have to offer the world, and get to know the world we're in. These two insights are essential if we hope to make an impression.

I love meeting new people, observing different ways of being in the world. It feeds me. It feeds my ideas. When I converse with people—again, I spend most of my day with the highest IQ and EQ leaders on the planet—I am endlessly intrigued to discover **their** patterns. More than this, I'm interested to observe their pure goodness—their inherent talents and observations. I want to get under their skin, to comprehend their composition, their unique gifts. And if I've taken the time to look deeply, to see them as they truly are, I get to glimpse their soul, the very essence of them.

I think music in itself is healing. It's an explosive expression of humanity. It's something we are all touched by.

Billy Joel, singer-songwriter and pianist

Soulfulness is an important part of the epic journey equation. If we don't invest what we do with soul, then it's never going to sing. When what we do is suffused with soul, miracles happen. As Lao Tzu, the ancient Chinese philosopher, once observed, "Music in the soul can be heard by the universe."

The essence of a life, to me, is the sound of one's own music. Who and what a person loves. How they see the world. How they want to make a difference. Every day, when we make the effort to learn and grow, more and more notes are added to our personal score. However, as former British Prime Minister Benjamin Disraeli noted, "Most people die with their music still locked up inside them." Whatever you do, please don't let your music die unheard.

Did you know that music comes from the Greek *mousikē*, meaning "art of the muses"? In times past, this was understood to be the inspirational goddesses of literature, science, and the arts, or simply as a person who serves as someone's source of artistic inspiration. Never doubt that there's plenty of inspiration out there.

If you're wanting to "make music," to add your unique voice and talents to the world, you need to get clear about what inspires you, what feeds your soul. Then spend time around the people and places that fill you, that can help propel you forward.

Many, many muses inspire me to activate my purpose every single day. Maybe I help inspire others to look inside themselves, as well to find meaning. I certainly hope so. The key is to understand the true value of the notes that live inside each muse, because once you have the notes, you become unstoppable. Or, as the classic movie *The Sound of Music* reminds us: Once we have found the right notes, we have a world of choices to sing from.

However, music isn't just about inspiration; it's about connectivity. When you can discern the notes within someone, you can then connect them and their notes to a perfect match. This connection point may be as simple as how someone thinks or acts, or how they faced similar traumatic childhoods. It may point to their roles as leaders. Or knowing someone's notes may suggest what types of connections they're seeking for investments, collaborations, or other needs. This process may even indicate whether two or more people have similar scores in their entrepreneurial goals or approaches.

Music is my secret weapon, and it can be yours too. Bruce Springsteen puts it well when he says, "The best music is essentially there to provide you something to face the world with." It has the capacity to lift us from where we are, to where we want to be.

Music is the great connector, and connecting people is what I do, what I love. It's how I live my life. How do I do this? I connect people by searching for the right note, the perfect note, to connect that one note to the next. We are all capable of doing this. Connection at its best creates a musical that never ends. A never-ending love story. How good is that?

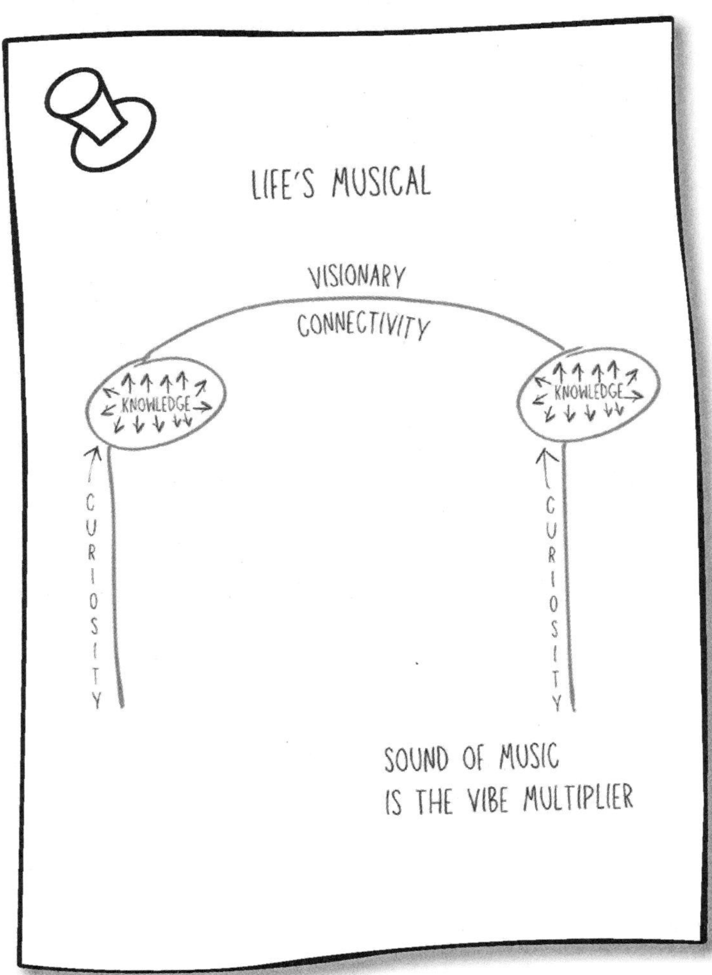
LIFE'S MUSICAL
VISIONARY
CONNECTIVITY
KNOWLEDGE
KNOWLEDGE
CURIOSITY
CURIOSITY
SOUND OF MUSIC
IS THE VIBE MULTIPLIER

EPIC TAKEAWAYS

- ✓ Think of connecting people as like writing a symphony, with each connection a musical note.
- ✓ Given music is a direct pathway to the heart, what music works for you?
- ✓ How can you add your unique notes, your unique talents, to the world?

STAY CURIOUS

THE GREATEST PEOPLE I've met have two fundamental traits. First, they are endlessly—and I do mean endlessly—curious. Second, they absolutely love acquiring knowledge from other endlessly curious people. None of my friends ever ask, "What do you do?" They are far more interested in learning who you are, who you love, and what your purpose is. They ask many more questions than they answer, and listen a great deal more than they speak. They know the music isn't just about them.

Curiosity is the wick in the candle of learning.

William Arthur Ward, motivational writer

An inquiring approach is about learning from others and putting those learnings into meaning, activation, and connection. To me, this is the highest form of art. Yet without a questioning mind, your ability to acquire knowledge and experience is diminished.

The combination of curiosity and knowledge creates endless connectivity because there are no limits to those learnings, those connections. The more curious a person, the more knowledge they acquire, and the more inquiring they become. This process is cyclical and musical. Life, at its best, is a constant quest to learn and share and connect more and more.

Let's not forget curiosity drives the exploration of science, of the world, of the self, and of others. And the payoff? There is no end to curiosity, no end to the benefits the questing mind can bring to the world, no end to the heights we can push ourselves to.

As Albert Einstein once said, "I am neither especially clever nor especially gifted. I am only very, very curious." While I don't believe that anyone could have revolutionized science the way Albert Einstein did, I've no doubt his exceptional intellect reached unimaginable heights in part because of his endless willingness to ask deep and searching questions.

According to *Psychology Today*, there are two types of curiosity: state and trait. State curiosity is defined as an individual's desire to acquire knowledge at a particular time. In contrast, trait curiosity is the characteristic of someone who is **constantly** interested in gaining knowledge and skills. People with trait curiosity can truly change the world.

Let's look at the research. When American psychologists, Todd Kashdan and John Roberts, conducted a study into curiosity, they found that those who exhibited trait curiosity had improved relationships with partners and that, in fact, trait curiosity was a clear predictor of those who enjoyed positive relationships with those around them.* Being curious about the world and other people

* Todd B. Kashdan and John E. Roberts, "Trait and State Curiosity in the Genesis of Intimacy: Differentiation from Related Constructs," *Journal of Social and Clinical Psychology* 23, no. 6 (2005), https://guilfordjournals.com/doi/abs/10.1521/jscp.23.6.792.54800?journalCode=jscp.

not only allows you to learn; it promotes better interactions with loved ones, colleagues, and acquaintances. And why wouldn't it? It feels good to be around those who are attuned to and interested in the world around them.

Another study into the effect of curiosity on work performance found that those who were inherently more curious about their work, and the world, had a better work output. The researchers concluded that workers who were more curious were more likely to be enthusiastic and to enjoy more positive experiences at work overall. This study concluded that "individuals who scored higher in curiosity performed better at work, which triggered them to experience more positive affect while working. These results indicate that curiosity boosts performance and workers' positive affect."*

These conclusions don't surprise me. I believe visionaries are those with boundless minds. They are endlessly curious about others and about their work. They are more able to express their vision out in the world and thus truly help others. Let's not forget that Socrates once said that "the unexamined life is not worth living." This is a great truth. If we do not push ourselves to expand our horizons and look more closely at our lives and the lives of others, we will miss out on the opportunity to lead a genuinely meaningful life.

The beautiful and interconnected nature of the planet's many cultures, countries, and peoples drives collaboration and, you guessed it, so too does curiosity. When we neglect this God-given skill to push out from what we already know and understand, we don't progress. We stay stuck, and so do those around us.

* Ana Junça-Silva and Daniel Silva, "Curiosity Did Not Kill the Cat: It Made It Stronger and Happy, but Only If the Cat Was Not 'Dark,'" *Acta Psychologica* 221, no. 103444 (2021), https://www.sciencedirect.com/science/article/pii/S0001691821001943.

Kids are born curious about the world. What adults primarily do in the presence of kids is unwittingly thwart the curiosity of children.

Neil deGrasse Tyson, astrophysicist and writer

If you're looking for inspiration, then look to the kids around you. Children are the most curious humans on this earth. While they have very limited knowledge about how or why the world works, they don't allow this to hold them back. They are constantly asking questions. Most parents would relate to the constant stream of "But, why?" questions they get.

Our children are the true visionaries of our world.

As annoying as this might be in a busy moment, the simple fact is that our kids are a clean slate. They're not yet restricted by a lifetime of stagnant beliefs. In Buddhism, this is known as the "beginner's mind," a treasured state of being. Why? Because a clean slate helps us access a multitude of possibilities. Never forget that our children are the true visionaries of our world. They are our future.

So, when kids ask, "But why is the sky blue?" six times in a row, we shouldn't respond, "I don't know, stop asking." Instead, we should research with them to figure out the answer. Who knows where this willingness to find a solution might lead? It may spark a lifetime of curiosity about people, architecture, or deep-sea diving. Perhaps one of our kids will grow up to become an astrophysicist, just like Neil deGrasse Tyson. The possibilities are endless.

Curiosity and knowledge-seeking are everything to me, whether through meeting those with boundless minds, or through experiential learning. When I have a gut feeling to ask or do something, I respect the wisdom of my gut and just do it, no questions asked.

Recently, I attended an event at a country club outside Wilmington, Delaware. Instead of driving to the venue, I decided to walk the five miles from downtown Wilmington, to get a sense of the difference between urban and rural living. For some reason, I just knew there was something special I was going to see.

As I left downtown Wilmington over the Washington Bridge, I had my answer on a plaque quoting George Washington: *May ample justice be done them here and may the choicest of heaven's favors, both here and hereafter, attend those who, under the divine auspices, have secured innumerable blessings for others.* What a powerful message. My heart exploded to witness this perfect description of how those with an expanded awareness are rewarded for their efforts, in blessing others with their actions and investments to create change in the world.

In among all our striving to make something of ourselves and our life, it's important to think about our legacy. What will each of us leave behind? Surely, we want to leave behind thoughts and ways of operating and structures that will live long past our time here—heartfelt efforts that inspire us, and that continue to inspire all those who know us, along with our children and their children, on and on through time. At its best, life is about creating powerful stepping stones that enable each to find their own journey.

Let's not forget that we maestros can compose anything we want. We can build any type of band, any orchestra, any note. Fired by our curiosity, we just have to keep asking questions, always seeking to expand our knowledge and helping us to keep forming meaningful connections that benefit ourselves and others.

EPIC TAKEAWAYS

- ✓ The true visionary thinks well beyond their own lifetime.
- ✓ Individuals, rather than large firms, are the leading factor in new knowledge creation. Think of yourself as your own knowledge creator.
- ✓ Every relationship represents an opportunity to learn and grow.

TRAUMA AND TRIUMPH

THERE'S AN OLD PARABLE about how things are not always what they seem. In the tale, a young boy walks through a farm and sees a sparrow that looks cold, hungry, and has a broken wing. The boy picks up the bird, covers its body in cow manure, looks for a tall branch, plants it firmly on the branch, and walks away. Two farmers who observed the boy's actions thought, "What a cruel young boy." However, when the farmers looked closer, they realized that the warmth of the cow manure was keeping the sparrow warm. Without it, the bird would have died from the cold. The sparrow was hungry, and the undigested pieces of grass satisfied its hunger. The manure became harder and harder, forming a splint. In the days to come, the bird's wing mended, and the sparrow was strong enough to fly away.

The point of the story is that not everything that happens to you is as it may seem, even if it puts you in a terrible, unpalatable, and dangerous situation. There may be karmic forces at play that, with your patience and your resources, will end up putting you in a better place than you could possibly have imagined.

Not everything that happens to you is actually what it seems.

José Saramago, winner of 1998 Nobel Prize in Literature

I tell you this story because, in 2017, after working as a journalist for more than twenty years and becoming an editor/reporter, I was called into the office and told my salary was being cut significantly. Two other reporters were fired that day. Twenty years down the drain in a five-minute meeting. It felt like I'd hit rock bottom.

I want you to reflect on a time when you have been in a similar situation. Were you unceremoniously fired from your job? Did a business venture go broke? Did a lover leave you for another? Did you think your school marks weren't good enough to get a degree? Think of the times in your life when you were like the little sparrow—hungry and cold, with a broken wing. Then, think about what helping hand came to assist you. What opportunities came your way to help you out of there?

For me, the little farm boy was my wife. She intuitively knew that if I had a change of scenery and environment after being devalued at work, it would allow me to regroup. So, she took me on a vacation. Like the little sparrow, I was put on a higher perch that allowed me a different view of the world. I was able to get off the ground and see things from a higher perspective.

You may think I'm fortunate to have a wife who could do this for me, but we all have friends, partners, and even strangers who cross our paths and give us a leg up. The universe moves in strange ways. There are silent sages, and there are individuals who give us a practical hand up. Sometimes, all we need is a kind word, a change of atmosphere, a different point of view.

BE OPEN TO ASSISTANCE THAT COMES FROM UNEXPECTED PLACES.

After having my salary cut and my wife taking me on vacation, I got the inspiration to start a PR agency. The firm serves as a connector for media opportunities. After starting up my first company, I had the inspiration to start a second company that connects any opportunity to any type of visionary.

So, be open to assistance that comes from unexpected places. The helping hand that reaches out to give you a lift up when you're at rock bottom may not come from someone you expect. Wisdom and insight can arise from the strangest places. Take me, for example. Most vacations are meant for relaxation. However, mine prompted me to think about setting up a business with no experience—which I can confidently say was not relaxing!

The change of scenery was what I needed to allow me to think outside the box I had created for myself, and it changed my life. So, stay open to support and guidance from everyone and everywhere, even when you don't expect it. It might just put you on a path you never knew you wanted to be on. The world has its own type of magic, the unexpected kind, where even a young farm boy can turn out to be someone's saving grace. Accept help, even from the strangest of places; it could be the world's magic trying to save you and put you on the right course.

For those fortunate to have partners, I strongly suggest that, instead of driving them away, you invite them into the process, because that's also part of their journey. They chose you. For those of you who can lean on friends and colleagues, look a little more closely. See if they are your farm boy. In any case, recognize that the farm boy is an individual who comes in and out of your life and offers help when you need it, because that's part of their karma.

This brings me to *The Seven Spiritual Laws of Success* by Dr. Chopra, in which he says, "Everyone has a purpose in life. A unique gift or special talent to give others." In my situation, and this will make you laugh, my former employers who cut my salary were the bearers of the most abundant gift for me. They kicked me out of the nest. They devalued my hard work. They didn't appreciate me enough. But they gave me the greatest gift, because they forced me to look for opportunities beyond them.

Like the little sparrow, Alphonso James was imprisoned in a lonely and dangerous place. Although his false imprisonment lasted for thirty-two years, he dug deep and remained extremely grateful. He said, "I had to go through extreme suffering in order to develop a deep sense of forgiveness and love." He describes his experience as one of "tremendous unimaginable suffering [and] a deep inner journey from rage, despair, and hatred, to love, purpose, and forgiveness." If that little sparrow could speak, there's no doubt he would chirp the same tune.

Most of us can relate to stories like that of the little sparrow, and to what James went through, though hopefully to a milder degree. At one stage, I met a man named Thomas Cernek, who was born and raised in the wilderness of tiny Mohawk, Michigan, a copper mine area of the Upper Peninsula. Cernek was a Navy hero who served in the Pacific and had the most dangerous role of any soldier. He has outlived all of his nine siblings. His wife of sixty-four years died earlier this decade, and he's outlasted all of his friends. Thomas has suffered great tragedy over and over, but he stays in the game. He has many grandchildren now. Shortly after our meeting, his first great-grandchild was born.

Visionaries never make excuses, even in the most difficult situations. A boundless person doesn't allow these setbacks to impede them or doesn't get lost in excuses. A boundless person knows that difficult situations are a necessary part of an enriched life.

I'm certain that the sparrow feels a bit foggy in the early morning, as do we. However, a lot of people don't enjoy change. They are happy to give into a fog that limits their view of the possibilities that life offers. Many people are trapped in the fog by their pride, their anger, their apathy, or their desire.

Whenever you experience a little fog in your life, think of the warmth of the sun, whose rays are well able to chase away any fogginess you may be experiencing. Boundless people transcend the fog, looking for opportunities and experiences outside of the mold that society has created.

I created the FOG Concept, which I believe encompasses most visionaries. To me, FOG stands for Faith, Obligation, and Glitches. Most boundless people have Faith in a higher power and in their ability to help others. They feel an Obligation to serve and improve the world, the real world that we live in. Boundless people must cause disruptions or Glitches in our regular way of life to get this change happening. The constant Obligation for true change is having the Faith to make it happen. Faith and the Obligation to create Glitches help to remove the FOG of the world and produce a revolutionary rebirth and enhanced evolution.

Like the little farm boy, not everyone who "puts you in the poo" is your enemy. I'm reminded of an article I read by Kazimierz Dabrowski, who died in 1980 after developing the Theory of Positive Disintegration. Dabrowski believed, "Conflict and inner suffering were necessary for advanced development—for movement toward a hierarchy of values based on altruism—for movement from 'what is' to 'what ought to be.'"

While conflict is necessary for us to develop and understand ourselves at a deeper level, this doesn't mean that we should deal with conflict on our own. I implore you to look for individuals who are there to support you, uplift you, and give you a different life perspective. Seek out those who encourage you to see your potential. You might be surprised by what you find. When you can see what special talents you have, and that you've been given a chance to excel, the next step is to become a helping hand and support others who have been kicked out of the nest.

While my PR firm was growing, many friends told me I needed to start a pure connectivity company, but I couldn't hold a pencil right—not kidding. Things that a monkey or child can do, I have a hard time doing. So, I needed to find a partner who could help me build a company. That was former cofounder, Mark Fujiwara. Mark was a great partner and connector, but we didn't have a firm plan to implement our vision, let alone put together the nuts and bolts of an organization to make a functioning company. That's when my wife came into the picture again. She saw that we were struggling and asked if she could serve as the company's integrator. I said yes, and now the company is thriving.

I implore you to look around and not try to do it all yourself. Part of the Law of Dharma is to blend your unique talents with the unique talents of others, to achieve a communal goal. Once you are successful and you're in a place where you're earning a comfortable income, then you can help others. I started my second company to connect people with those who can help them achieve their dreams. This follows the Law of Dharma: As you prosper, you will enable others to prosper, which in turn makes you more prosperous.

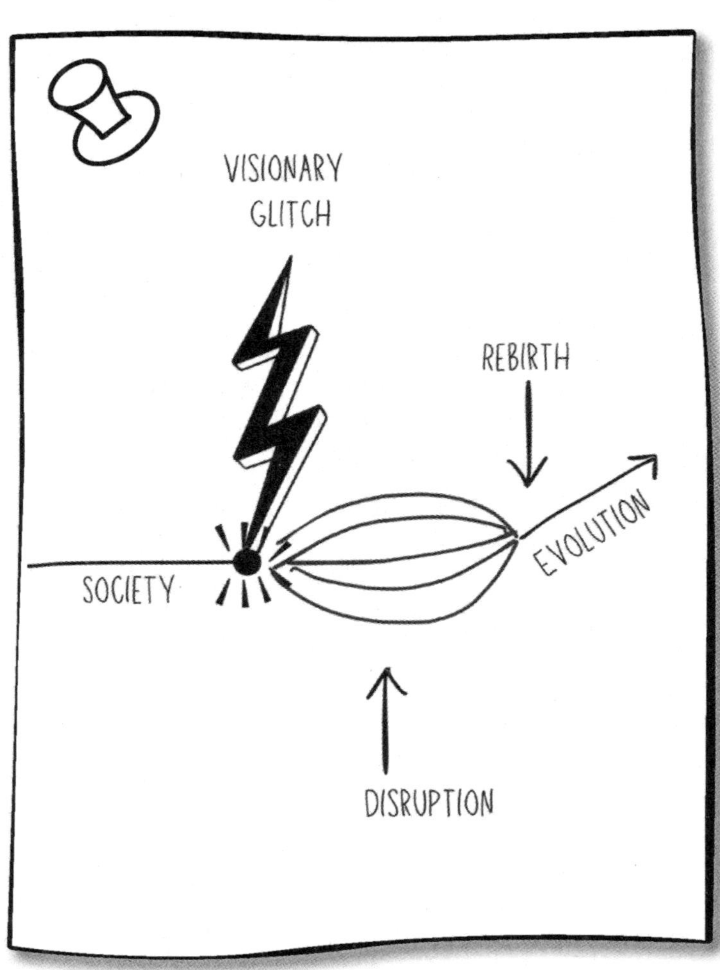
VISIONARY
GLITCH
REBIRTH
SOCIETY
EVOLUTION
DISRUPTION

EPIC TAKEAWAYS

- ✓ Not every catastrophe in your life is a catastrophe.
- ✓ Accept assistance and support from others without reservation.
- ✓ When you do emerge from a catastrophe, help someone else.
- ✓ Look beyond the fog and reframe it to "Faith, Obligation, Glitches."
- ✓ Work with people whose attributes complement yours, or who have attributes that you lack.

NOURISH YOURSELF, NOURISH YOUR VISION

SO, YOU HAVE A BURNING DESIRE to change what needs changing in your slice of the world. You yearn to make a difference, a real difference, but you're finding the journey exceedingly lonely and hard. You've become a Lone Ranger, someone who's got used to doing things on their own. There are times in our journey when we need to walk alone, but it can become a habit, a bad habit, which can easily tip us into survival mode.

When we go it alone, our capacity for boundless thinking and action recedes, as does our ultimate vision. True vision needs a lot of good input. It needs to be fertilized by a whole grab bag of fresh ideas, input, and enthusiasm from others. Why? Because none of us knows what we don't know. Sometimes all it takes is a chance comment, an off-the-wall suggestion, or throwaway line to transform how we're doing things.

Wil Schroter, who has launched nine start-ups over three decades and more, wrote the following in an article titled "Why Founders Don't Ask for More" for startups.com:

> As Founders, we tend to spend all of our time helping others or, at the very least, fixing everyone else's problems. That has a lot to do with being at the top of the org chart, where there's kind of nowhere else to go with our problems. Everyone else can defer to us to make a decision, but the buck kinda stops there. Like anything in life, it becomes a habit [to go it alone]. We're getting used to having to have the answer every time. We get used to being the final word. If we do anything in life long enough, we quickly forget that there's any other way.

Not everyone is into launching start-ups. You may have a community project, a local charity, a fundraiser dear to your heart—a goal so precious that you give it everything you have, and then some, because it means so much to you. You give and give until you exhaust yourself and still you keep on giving, not seeing that you're now dragging yourself around in ever diminishing circles, not noticing that your vision is shrinking too. We can get so caught up in our goals, in doing the work, that we forget to feed our hearts and nourish our souls. Essential parts of us recede because, without meaning to, we compromise everything we're capable of.

To keep your dreams alive, you also need to nourish the dreamer. That means taking time out to breathe, to step back a little, to recalibrate. Don't be shy about asking for assistance, and not just with the basics. It's important to ask for help in keeping your vision on track. Talk to a range of trusted people. Listen to and work with their responses. That way your precious project is less likely to become tired or off track.

The beautiful African American writer and activist, Maya Angelou, points the way saying, "My mission in life is not merely to survive, but to thrive; and to do so with some passion, some compassion, some humor, and some style." Note that compassion sits alongside passion here. Passion is a great motivator, great fuel for our path, but we can so easily lose perspective by pushing ourselves and those who come along for the journey too hard, unless we keep a clear eye.

Compassion takes the hard edges off our passion to succeed. Compassion infuses our efforts with breadth and depth and humanity. Compassion is inclusive, kind, and generous. It expands what we're capable of. It draws others to us. It lights the way by activating unexpected moments of synchronicity. It widens the possibilities ahead, enabling us to step into the fullest and best version of what we seek to create.

Part of stepping back is getting into the habit of looking at new ways to operate in the world. Here, I'm indebted to my friend and boundless thinker, Smoke Wallin, who works with labyrinths. This powerful, ancient technology is enjoying a revival, as people discover the very real benefits of labyrinths. "The Labyrinth opens one to the wisdom of the universe through a simple pattern of one way in and one way out," Smoke explains. He adds, "Holding in mind an intention or important question, and contemplatively doing the Labyrinth, pausing in the center for a bit, then returning to the entry, opens a pathway to divinity and can bring peace, inspiration, and answers."

Considerable research has been conducted into the effects of labyrinths, captured by The Labyrinth Society. Almost three-quarters of participants in one study reported feeling "much less" or "less" anxious following their labyrinth walk. Others talk of "calming, meditative states that open one up to one's intuitive, creative nature, and allow for a shift in consciousness." Sixty-four percent of labyrinth walkers reported feeling "much more" or "more" open following their labyrinth walk, while 74 percent of participants felt "much more" or "more" peaceful prior to entering the maze.

In summary, it appears that "walking or otherwise interacting with the labyrinth might enable a set of physical responses that [in turn] allows for the emergence of a set of 'state of mind' responses . . . [that] might increase one's receptivity to flashes of intuition, hunches, nudges from one's 'inner voice,' and other types of insight regarding one's problems, issues, or concerns."*

The term "labyrinth" comes from the Latin *laborintus* meaning a maze, a great building with many corridors and turns. Intriguingly, the labyrinth is also a complex structure in the inner ear, which contains the organs of hearing and balance. It consists of bony cavities filled with fluid and is lined with sensitive membranes.

Put simply, a labyrinth is the name of the structure of the inner ear, the essential organ of hearing. Let's focus here on the balance and hearing aspects of a labyrinth. First, let's take a walk figuratively speaking, by simply contemplating what the labyrinth might offer us in terms of a subtle opening up inside, a shift in consciousness.

Having taken these benefits on board, why not try a labyrinth walk for yourself? You may be lucky enough to have a labyrinth within reach, as there are currently some 6,400 labyrinths across the planet. If you're unable to access a physical labyrinth don't worry, you can still enjoy similar effects by drawing a labyrinth contemplatively. While you're completing your drawing, be sure to pause in the center of the labyrinth and allow for

* John W. Rhodes, "Commonly Reported Effects of Labyrinth Walking," in *Labyrinth Pathways* (2nd ed.), 31–37.

whatever clarification you're needing to come to you, in a way that works for you.

In his book, *Create Yourself*, Ivan Rhodes describes the labyrinth as "an archetypal collective symbol grounded in consciousness itself, a journey into your own Self." What more precious gift can we give ourselves, amid all we strive to achieve, than to have the opportunity to access our True-Self? Or, as my friend Smoke, who first introduced me to the immense benefits of the labyrinth, pointed out in one of our many conversations:

> The Labyrinth opens one to the wisdom of the universe through a simple pattern with one way in and one way out. Holding in mind an intention or important question and contemplatively doing the Labyrinth, pausing in the center for a bit, then returning to the entry opens a pathway to divinity and can bring peace, inspiration, and answers.

On my wider journey of self-discovery, I've also been drawn to the work of Nancy Ann Tappe, a sixties parapsychologist and psychic, who began to notice children with indigo auras. Her work would later be expanded by Lee Carroll and Jan Tober. These indigo children, Nancy noted, were clearly different. Intuitive and intelligent, empathic and curious, they had a clear sense of self and purpose, and an innate spiritual bent from early childhood. I can't fully explain why yet, but the word "Nancy" keeps resounding in my head. This will no doubt be revealed to me in the fullness of time.

Meanwhile, let's dive a little deeper into the indigo phenomenon. Interestingly, if you shift the letters of the word around, you get "God in I." That alone is enough to give us pause. Set between true

1
GOD SPEED
YOUR LOVE
TO ME
G
O
E
S
B
Y
CARRY EACH OTHER
ONE
TIME
CAN DO SO MUCH

blue and violet, indigo is the color of the last blue sky before true nightfall. One article in *Medium*, an online publishing platform, describes indigo as the "king of blues." This arresting color, first used as a dye in the Harappan Valley in 3300 BC, has massive longevity. "Once dyed it will not fade away unless very strong detergents are used on it or if it is exposed to prolonged sunlight. . . . The natural indigo dye is so amazing that it does not require a mordant (the substance that will ensure the dye stays on fabrics) and it is a chemical-free process."*

In terms of our chakras, the living vortexes of energy inside us, indigo relates to the third eye in the middle of our forehead. As the seat of our sixth sense, its deeper vision allows us to connect more profoundly and insightfully with ourselves, with the world around us and, crucially, to the Divine. Our third eye assists in a deepening of our consciousness, by enabling us to intuitively sense what's going on in and around us, at a far deeper level than we could access through our five senses.

When we can access this level of insight and nurture, it becomes natural for us to operate more effectively in the world, to supercharge the goals we hold in our heart. With this level of guidance, no one else needs to be hurt along the way. It's no difficulty for us to be kind, responsible, and respectful when we're genuinely connected to ourselves, to each other, to our higher selves. It's easier too to see beauty in the world wherever we find it, to honor it rather than exploit it, and this includes our interactions with women.

The only directive I had about scaling our company was that we had to have the highest percentage of women possible. I was tired of being in rooms of mostly men, driven by ego and IQ, but lacking heart, especially when seeing what's happening currently—the devastating ways this lack of heart is impacting humanity. This is

* Desihands.com, "Indigo – The Most Beautiful Blue Ever", Medium, June 14, 2016.

not a time on the planet purely for ego and intelligence, not unless it's infused by heart.

This is not a time on the planet purely for ego and intelligence, not unless it's infused by heart.

To achieve this, we need to truly value the power of the feminine. It's essential we start to see the women in our lives in their wholeness, and not just how they look. As iconic movie legend Audrey Hepburn reminds us:

> The beauty of a woman is not in the clothes she wears, the figure that she carries, or the way she combs her hair. The beauty of a woman is seen in her eyes, because that is the doorway to her heart, the place where love resides. True beauty in a woman is reflected in her soul. It's the caring that she lovingly gives, the passion that she shows.

Right now, the world is crying out for the sheer magic and nurture of the feminine principle, which perfectly complements all that male energy offers. Shortly, we'll deep dive into the legend of Poseidon and Amphitrite, the story of Poseidon the great God of the Sea who, on glimpsing the lovely Amphitrite, searched the world over for her. Having witnessed her beauty, he knew intuitively he was incomplete without her.

When we embrace our feminine selves, we are transformed. Our power is amplified, because it is tempered with kindness. So too is responsibility, when accompanied by a willingness to laugh at ourselves. In part, the gift of the feminine is in realizing the journey is less about being afraid to be wrong, than to be inauthentic. It's about finding the courage to make a place at the table for those who are different. The ability to dance with success as well as failure, to find time to sit and contemplate, as well as to strive.

However, before we can truly connect with others, it's important we create an ever-deepening relationship with our true selves in the many ways already discussed. As singer-songwriter Kurt Cobain reminds us, "Wanting to be someone else is a waste of the person you are."

EPIC TAKEAWAYS

- ✓ Accepting compliments and asking for help are essential tools on the journey.
- ✓ Remember, a labyrinth is also the structure of the inner ear, an essential organ of hearing.
- ✓ Find commonalities and potential partnerships in those who are as misunderstood as you are.
- ✓ We are here to live life, not just exist.

TRUST—WRONG ROADS, RIGHT DESTINATIONS

The road to success is always under construction.

Lily Tomlin

IT'S MAY 16, 2024, and I've just completed a four-mile run as the sun rose over Phoenix, Arizona. The reds, oranges, and golds of the desert dawn reminded me of the city's mythological namesake. The phoenix is an immortal bird that cyclically regenerates. It is a powerful symbol of rebirth, of rising anew from ashes.

The roads we take and the directions they take us may feel like lifetimes. Walking from the ashes and into an unknown future with trust takes courage. But when we do so, even the wrong roads can lead us to promising destinations, as we emerge in the right places through serendipity, through unexpected possibilities opening up for us.

I listen to music when I run and from this morning's playlist, the above Foo Fighter's lyric still echoes in my ears. "Everlong" is fitting for a chapter reflecting on trust and the spirit of the phoenix. Let's sing along together as I share the lessons, stories, and insights from yesterday—one of the most transformative days of my life.

Yesterday marked the first in-person meeting of the Epic F.I.T. Network. It was a convergence of **F**low, **I**kigai (a Japanese concept meaning "a reason to live"), and **T**rue-Self (the principles that define our mission and inspired our new company name). The room was filled with the vibrant energy of individuals driven by purpose. As someone who typically avoids big group settings, preferring a quiet corner near the exit, I was surprised to find myself fully immersed in the event.

My friend, Richard Canfield, an electric presence who walks on a treadmill during virtual meetings, sat beside me. Right before the event began, I shared the title of this chapter with him, because he had said these words which stuck with me during a previous meetup: "Wrong Roads, Right Destination." Their sentiment had stayed with me and, over the course of the day, have proved their wisdom many times over.

The paths that had brought us all together for that moment were varied and unpredictable, but their convergence was beautiful. The day was marked by profound connection and creation. Relationships deepened and expanded in ways that transcended the surface.

One of our members, Dr. Kien Vuu, gave an incredible presentation. Dr. V., as he's affectionately known, was the lone baby to survive the passage with thousands of Vietnamese refugees on a freighter ship in the 1970s. His journey from survival to success is nothing short of extraordinary. In America, Kien Vuu grew up to become a doctor who was overweight and depressed. He then chose a different road for himself and is now a husband, father, and one of the top performance optimization and longevity experts on the planet. He talked about his young daughter, Kaia, who barely survived birth when the umbilical cord wrapped around her neck, and who subsequently spent a great deal of time in the ICU.

This prompted Dr. Vuu to simplify his life into four transformative statements, which we can all benefit from:

1. The power of choice is ours.
2. How we live our life is medicine.
3. I met a man who was about to die, who reminded me how to live.
4. Identity is a choice, not a condition.

Dr. Vuu's lessons resonated as a reminder that when we face our choices with courage and trust, serendipity will lead us—our destinations become our destiny.

My friend Melissa Bernstein, who has a gift for combining concepts that open new meanings and pathways of understanding, is a great blessing to me. Being with her is like blending letters to form a new toy for our minds to play with and explore. Recently, she introduced me to two words to help us reframe how we perceive challenges:

1. **Blurse** = blessing + curse. Most things are a combination of both. When we mine our curses for their blessings, we can better realize our full potential.
2. **Traumeaning** = trauma + meaning. This is about mining traumas to determine how they happened **for** us, rather than **to** us. When we become self-aware and objective enough to do this, we attain a new level of enlightenment.

These two words, simple yet profound, highlight the potential within life's dualities. Trusting that there is meaning and growth to be found in all our experiences, both blessings and challenges, is a trait of boundlessness. With this perspective comes surprising avenues for understanding and transformation.

It was a marvel to watch these ideas take flight and release the buzz that came from numerous personal tales of resilience, resourcefulness, and renewal. In mining trauma, we find more than meaning. We release hidden stores of courage and trust.

Melissa shared with me a powerful concept:

> Once you've mastered the rules, then you must **reject** everything you know and start over again with a completely blank slate. You must bring yourself to the domain and see it with completely new eyes. That space is where novelty is conceived.

Trusting ourselves to let go of what we know and embracing the unknown requires immense courage—a "phoenix heart." It's in that vulnerable space of starting anew that true innovation and growth occur. Yesterday, as we brainstormed, created, and collaborated, I witnessed the sharing of these principles as an unfolding of dharma, a blossoming of wisdom-lead actions and support. The meeting was never about networking or business strategies. It was about aligning with Flow, discovering our Ikigai, and embracing our True-Self. It was about connecting to the essence of what makes life meaningful.

Flow is the state of being fully present, trusting the moment to unfold as it should. Ikigai is the joy found in living with purpose. True-Self is the authenticity that emerges when we trust in our journey. These principles weren't just discussed yesterday. They were lived.

The sun over Phoenix has now fully risen and that Foo Fighters' song still echoes. I'm reminded of Gregory David Roberts, who suggests that there are no mistakes. Only new paths to explore. I can only smile, as the wrong roads and right directions have shown me that with trust and flow, yes, life can feel that real. The thread that weaves together roads and destinations is the courage to mine meaning from challenges, to start anew, and to align with our true purpose.

Own your phoenix heart, knowing that renewal is always possible. Trust in the process and find yourself exactly where you need to be.

EPIC TAKEAWAYS

- ✓ The power of choice is yours. Trust yourself to make decisions that align with your purpose.
- ✓ Trust in the hidden blessings within challenges.
- ✓ Reject the rules and embrace the blank slate.
- ✓ When life takes you to all the right places, don't waste time begrudging the road that brought you there. Celebrate your arrival—be boundless.

DEATH, LIFE, AND LOVE

THE LAST TIME I SAW MY DAD was a Monday morning, when I was in the eighth grade. The principal pulled me out of class, and my best friend's mom drove me to the hospital. My dad had suffered a catastrophic heart attack. He managed to stay conscious long enough to say goodbye to me and my two younger brothers. His last words before slipping into a coma were, "My boys!" A few days later, on January 18, 1991, he was gone.

We live just two blocks away from that hospital, and I run past it six or seven times a week. The sight always stirs echoes of that day and is a constant reminder that death is part of life.

Years later, my youngest brother, Jerry, passed away at the age of twenty-nine. His life had unraveled to a quiet end in a dingy hotel room in Florida. A PhD student who played concert piano, Jerry was brilliant. But his final moments were spent alone with his opioid addiction. My middle brother, Doug, was there when Jerry's body was wheeled out in a body bag. It was a cruel and unimaginable moment. Jerry is now buried next to our dad, in a plot that was meant for our mother.

When I think of death, an earlier loss stands out as the most painful. I'd watched, helpless, as our malamute/shepherd puppy chased a rabbit across the street and was struck by a truck. This pain was overwhelming, unexpected, and difficult for my young self to comprehend. Molly was beautiful, innocent, and full of life, and then she was gone. My brothers and I held her as she died, and then our neighbor helped us to put her in a black garbage bag ready for cremation. It still seems surreal and will always be heart-wrenching.

I'm not afraid of death because death is part of life—and I'm not afraid of life. I don't believe we fully die while our memories and lessons are passed on. My dad, my brother, and our sweet puppy Molly live on. Explicitly, such as being part of this book, and implicitly, as their presence in my life is intertwined with the memories and lessons I share with others. In this way, most of life's great lessons have been immortalized in writing or in memory. They are accessible—all we need to do is find them.

I feel incredibly lucky to have come from a family of historians and lifelong learners. Perhaps the greatest example of this is my dad's World War II diary. His entries were written during the worst days of the Battle of Hürtgen Forest, a harrowing part of World War II, the kind of bloody chaos that's been immortalized in films like *Fury*. My dad's writings and sketches continue to be a source of inspiration and insight.

Dad's entry from New Year's Eve, 1944, is particularly potent. Only moments after the gruesome death of a squad mate, he was assigned to fly a mission. Walt, Dad's flight partner, was still green with nausea after what they had witnessed, but they flew:

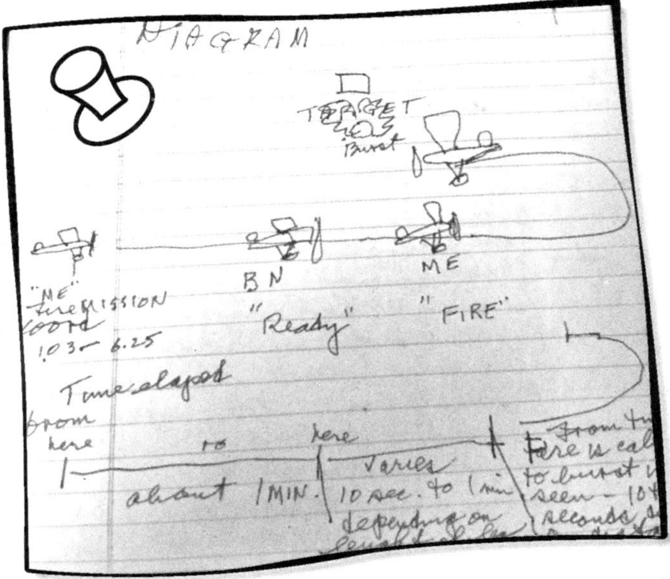

The strain is telling on Walt, but I don't want to pass up the opportunity to shoot up these targets. There is a lot of tension and feeling involved in going up on a mission immediately after seeing one of your men killed in a crash and I can appreciate what Walt is going through.

After two hours in the air, the mission is deemed a success.

Then it dawns on us that this is New Year's Eve. What with all that's happened today, nobody feels like celebrating, although most of the guys could use a shot of whiskey to steady them . . . Well, tomorrow, a new year starts, and we're wondering what it will bring and how many of us will be around throughout the year.

This ability to live each and every moment is my litmus test for a life well lived. There are no excuses for not embracing the boundlessness within. We could die at any moment. My dad was lucky to survive the war, to die in a hospital ward years later. That said, there are no guarantees outside the present. Did you know the word "gift" comes from the Latin *praesent,* meaning "being at hand"? There's a clue for making the most of the now. Be hands-on.

The treasures hidden in my dad's journal stay with me, reminding me of the fragility of life, and the bravery required to keep moving forward with this awareness. In the Woody Allen film, *Midnight in Paris,* Gertrude Stein says, "We all fear death and question our place in the universe. The artist's job is not to succumb to despair, but to find an antidote for the emptiness of existence."

I believe this to be true. We are all, in some ways, artists of our own lives—creating meaning where there might otherwise be none. Through love, through our relationships, and through the work we do, we find purpose. In the same film, Ernest Hemingway's character says, "I believe that love that is true and real, creates a respite from death. All cowardice comes from not loving or not loving well, which is the same thing."

The meaning of life is to love and be a witness to it.

Heather Wagenhals, author and TV talk show host

Likewise, we also find comfort in love. Love pushes death aside, if only for a moment. Through love, the awareness of death and the pain or fear of potential endings grow stronger. And in this, the immediacy of life is magnified. Each moment becomes a portal for boundlessness. Death, we come to realize, is a precious and important part of life's equation.

It's not a fascination with death, but a testimony to my joy of the moment, that inspired me to follow best-selling author Donald Miller's advice in *Hero on a Mission* and write my own eulogy. This document is not so much about how I wish to be remembered, but how I want to define myself. It is a mission statement that I can turn to in life. Regardless of what is going on, it's up to me to fly the plane. At the end of each day, I want to be able to tell myself, "He lived a meaningful life and created true meaning for others. And he always followed his heart to find the truest love possible, even if it meant risking it all to find it."

But what exactly does it mean to live with meaning? I've asked my closest friends how they define meaning. My friend Heather Wagenhals says it best: "The meaning of life is to love and be a witness to it, so that the object of your affections knows intimately how much they mattered."

Yes, love makes life meaningful. That's why my wife and my children are in the opening line of my eulogy. They provide me with a life I never thought was possible. They are the key players in my greatest memories and experiences. Yet while love gives us meaning, it's also important not to live through our objects of affection. As Johnny Poulsen, cofounder and CEO of Income Lab, said, "Live **with** your children, not **through** them."

When I share this quote with other parents, they usually respond with, "Well, obviously." However, it's clear that many people do live through their kids, to some degree or other. According to *Inc. magazine* and researchers from Utrecht University in Holland, this may be due to unresolved disappointment from the past. Their study found that when we feel pride and fulfillment in our children's glory, it can help heal those emotional wounds in the present.

This is where being a witness to ourselves—our thoughts, feelings, and emotions—can take us to greater fulfillment. When we are not engaging with others merely to understand, heal, or realize ourselves, but in the service of **greater** meaning, we step into the wisdom of dharma. The magazine article concludes with the sentiment that "mentally strong parents raise mentally strong kids."

When we live each moment as boundless, it is not possible to live through anyone else, including our children. We become examples of how to live. Our strengths, our passions, and our boundlessness influence and inspire our children and all those we encounter.

EPIC TAKEAWAYS

- ✓ Life is fleeting and fragile, so be hands-on and delve into every moment with love and awareness.
- ✓ Life, death, and love are interconnected.
- ✓ Press forward in the face of impermanence, strong in love, inspired to be a living example of authenticity and boundlessness.

ABUNDANCE APEX

AT ITS HIGHEST EXPRESSION, abundance is life-enhancing, nourishing, and always seeks the greatest good for ourselves and for others. Manifesting sacred abundance, abundance informed by our Higher Self, is our soul's true calling. Everything else is incidental. Why? Because life, because each day, is infinitely precious. Too precious to waste on selfish goals.

Like it or not, our lives are finite. That's why our choices matter, and thanks to the infinite wisdom of the universe, there are plentiful markers along the way should we choose to take note of them.

Markers have a way of coming out of nowhere. They have a way of elevating our consciousness in the moment. My son Chase and I went to pizza one night, when he was eight. We were talking about IQ and bending time, simple stuff really, when Chase admitted that he sees life as one long, great day. Yesterday, he explained, is before you're born, and tomorrow is after you die. He went on to say there are only two ways to have a long, great day. First, create more living things (another human, planting a tree, a foundation, etc.). Second, do what you like to do and what you're good at (follow your passions) and keep getting better at them. Chase is a simplifier like me, but a much better human being.

Chase also understands the value of consciousness, and how geometry has the power to unlock and raise our deepest awareness, to point the way forward. Like the sages of old, he realizes the importance of math and shapes, how geometry is part of the timeless language of sacred guidance. How does this work? He and I were talking about how triangles serve as the strongest shape, noting that bridges are constructed of triangles. In contemplating a triangle's inherent strength, Chase and I see the best bridges, and partnerships, as triangular.

Let me explain. As we reflected earlier, the biggest issue the world faces right now is that most capital, especially venture capital, is controlled by men with ego—Father Suns, self-obsessed, destructive individuals.

However, to create a life of worth, we need balance. Life was never meant to be just about us. This balance comes from combining Father Sun **and** Mother Earth, by incorporating the feminine element into what we do, as we discussed earlier. Chase describes Mother Earths as the source of life and reflection. This is an important insight, because while there are times when we need to forge ahead, there are also times when we need to pause and reflect, if we're to stay on track. It's the dance of the Yin and Yang, reflection and action.

Chase also recognizes that sometimes Neutral Moons take on sun energy, and at other times take on Mother Earth energy. This then forms a triangular structure that's inherently robust yet fluid, a structure where the load is **shared**. The triangle is also a universal, cosmic work of geometrical art. A beautiful bridge.

The triangle also represents the number three in sacred geometry—signifying the unity of the head, heart, and gut and also of the light, spirit, and soul. A life lived in harmony with our head, heart, and gut enables us to elevate all we're capable of, infusing all our actions with the wisdom of the Divine. Informed by the light, by the purest expression of our human spirit and our soul's true wisdom, we get to access the highest possibilities for our creativity and self-expression. This is how we get to serve ourselves and others in ways that genuinely heal, uplift, and inspire. We get to re-vision all we're capable of, to elevate our offerings.

I know this to be true. The PR firm I established has thrived, but I see now its main role has been to lead me to create the second company, which is essentially about the highest form possible of connectivity for others. It's a Software as Service Platform, which creates events and media, a philanthropic and education universe, for all those seeking to free themselves from the conditioned mind and embrace an enhanced, boundless creativity, in service to the needs of the planet.

My sole and soul purpose in life now is to connect those with a higher vision to serve humanity. My new company does this, and will continue to do this, at the highest level possible. Its goal? To truly change the world. My PR firm serves as a connector for media opportunities. This second company generates endless possibilities for those who prefer to live and operate out of the square.

Interestingly, others could see this was where I needed to be heading before I could. While the PR firm was growing, many friends told me I needed to start a pure connectivity company, but as I said previously, I can't hold a pencil right. Things that even a monkey or child can do, I have a hard time doing. So, I needed to find a partner who could unpack my vision and make it a reality. That was my former brilliant cofounder, Mark Fujiwara.

The second company was incorporated in April 2021. Mark is a great connector. While we had countless amazing contacts between us, we didn't have a plan to turn our vision into reality. We needed someone to help us ensure this new venture was a high-functioning machine, well able to deliver on its promise. That's where my wife, Mother Earth, came into the picture. Dr. Sarah saw us struggling and, during a couples retreat in California, asked if she could serve as the company's integrator/COO.

I was shocked because, at the time, Dr. Sarah was a full-time pediatrician. Our first date was the day before she started medical school. At the time she made this offer, we had two young, very wild sons, and she had zero experience running a company. Trusting the wisdom of my gut, I said, "Great idea! Makes perfect sense!"

When Sarah took over in May 2023, we had six members and no true platform. Currently we have seventy-five members, a SAAS site and app, three to four virtual meetings a month, and a big in-person event coming up in Arizona. In addition, we've just started our own TV channel with thirty-million-plus reach and are collaborating with one of our members to launch an MBA program for our members, again focused on raising consciousness. We were honored to be named one of the top five new masterminds on the planet by *Business Traveler USA Magazine*.

For the record, I have **nothing** to do with the nuts and bolts of what we do. That's all down to Sarah and others working together. That's not my skill set. If I tried to do what Sarah and her team accomplish, I'd melt the company. Sometimes, I'll pop into one of Sarah's Zoom meetings with her amazing assistant Pam to see what they're doing, and then they nicely (sometimes not nicely) ask me to leave.

My skill is building networks. Tying my shoes isn't easy, so I had to learn how to build things using the connectivity powers of my heart, brain, and soul.

So how does this relate to the Abundance Apex? When we move into deep alignment with our soul's true purpose, life cooperates, signaling opportunities ahead and linking soul paths for the wider good. We connect into a deeper expression of abundance, that of seeking to raise the vibrations of the planet. And in response, the universe helps you and I make it happen, whatever the "it" is for you. Your calling may be local, focused on community, or it may be global. Both add value. The principles are the same.

Let me explain. Five years back, Mike Malatesta, a man of true foresight, sent me a LinkedIn message. He'd heard me on Steve Sims's podcast and had enjoyed the stories and wisdom I shared. Mike and I started communicating. He invited me on his podcast. We talked about life, family, and many other things. Mike then became a PR partner. My firm simplified his story, then shared it with other out-of-the-box thinkers on their shows.

Mike and I became close. Eventually he invited me on his show again, where we talked about a phrase I used to use as my email signature: *Abundance Mentality Is the Only Mentality!* Seeing this, Mike suggested I join an entrepreneur group he's part of called Abundance 360, led by Dr. Peter Diamandis. An essential part of the group's mindset is the belief that the world is endlessly abundant, with limitless possibilities for those who choose to live that way. It's about choosing to grow every single day, instead of staying fixed.

I joined. I already knew I wanted to create a connectivity platform, but didn't know how, or who would help me. I was chatting with Dan Sullivan, cofounder of Strategic Coach®, one of the greatest entrepreneurial coaches ever. During our virtual conversation, I said I needed to "find my Babs," as Dan's wife Babs, cofounder of Strategic Coach®, has helped grow the business to serve thousands.

Dan replied, "The trick is having your Babs find you." His comment intrigued me. I liked the idea of allowing synchronicity into the equation. Later that day, I used their Strategic Coach® tool, an "Impact Filter®," to flesh out what my connectivity company would look like in ten years. Impact Filter® gave me a much-needed structure. It helped me get a sense of the road ahead. Everything I wrote then has pretty much happened.

After getting to know Dr. Diamandis, I asked him if he'd write the foreword for my book *Epic Life*. He agreed. Peter is remarkable, as is his family history. His late father was the first in his family to leave the Greek island of Lesvos—where he fed goats and picked olives—to come to America and achieve his dream of becoming a physician. When on stage at A360, Peter always thanks his family, especially his mom. He won an Estes Rocket Design Competition when he was twelve years old, and to me, he's still that curious kiddo winning model rocket contests.

As always, I like to pay attention to the "notes" others vibrate at. It's like a cosmic form of connectivity, where I'm guided towards those I feel aligned with. That's how I met the talented James Bly (through A360). He introduced me to Doug Holladay, a brilliant man and founder of PathNorth, which "aims to inspire a community of leaders to explore ways to bring greater meaning to both life and work." When I asked Doug for his purpose, he simply said "to find and promote meaning."

Doug invited me to a PathNorth event. Here Roosevelt Giles, the son of cotton-picking sharecroppers and now a partner at NASDAQ among many other things, stood out. During one of our subsequent discussions, Roosevelt asked me to speak about my book *Epic Life* to the Stakeholder Impact Foundation Group he chairs, a group dedicated to "delivering transformative change through full participation of diverse leadership." Then he invited

JUST capital
SHAKE & BAKE
SHAKE & BAKE

me to help ring the closing bell at NASDAQ. How could I say no?

At the NASDAQ event, I met Dr. Chopra, chairman emeritus of Just Capital. The company was being honored at the bell-ringing ceremony. He is pure kindness and consciousness. Just being in his presence is an immense gift. He embodies the Abundance Apex to a level I'd never experienced before.

A few weeks later, a sudden glitch landed, urging me to share recent experiences in this book. I felt an overwhelming urge to see if Dr. Chopra would write an introduction for this book, so I spoke to Shelby Joy Scarbrough, an accomplished friend and former PR partner and member of our connectivity company. Remarkably, she had just talked to one of Dr. Chopra's partners, Rajesh Setty, who . . . wait for it . . . is also a member of our connectivity platform. I arranged a call with Rajesh, also an author of many books, whose passion is "to bring good and game-changing ideas to life with love."

This is one example of the countless connection bridges that spiderweb through my heart and head. It's what happens when we seek the highest purpose in an endeavor, thereby unlocking our Abundance Apex. All we need is to step into alignment and trust, then be prepared to act, because the cooperation we get from the universe doesn't stop, ever, even during dreams. In fact, insights and problem-solving increase exponentially when I'm asleep. Maybe my oldest son Jake is spot-on when he says that we're awake when we're asleep, and we're asleep when we're awake.

I always wondered if there was a point where my brain or heart couldn't handle this level of connectivity, but I'm sure because of the glitches/disruption/rebirth/evolution there will never be a limit on the abundant ideas and possibilities life sends our way, even well after body death.

I know you too have sparks and glitches to remind you to connect to people for no apparent reason, which eventually become incredibly apparent and powerful. Be grateful for these glitches. Act on them and see where they take you. Often, they will come out of left field. That's often a good sign you're on track, because cosmic abundance takes you beyond the obvious. If there's someone you really are thinking about right now, reach out to them **right now**. Don't hesitate. There is a reason they're in your heart and mind.

One of my father's favorite sayings was: *The cream rises to the top*. I used to think this meant climbing the journalism ladder or becoming an elite entrepreneur, husband, and dad. I now see that to reach the Abundance Apex, you must rise through the most suffering, the most commitment, the most effort. Ultimately, whatever divinely inspired suffering, discomfort, and dislocation we face is a matter of alchemy. Over time, as we continue to strive to perfect the perfection in us, our hardships are transformed into our greatest soul pleasures. We get to see it's an honor to serve the higher power, which controls whatever happens anyway. It's the only way to reach enlightenment.

Mike, who I mentioned earlier, is a great example of having to do the hard yards to grow, to succeed. His media résumé includes the following:

> In Mike Malatesta's first ten years as an entrepreneur, he had been indicted, lost an employee, and lost a business partner in a fatal fire in one of his own company's facilities. He eventually decided that everything that happened to him was only one person's fault: his own.

If we want to operate at the highest level of integrity, there can be no excuses, only action and investment, then taking responsibility for our actions and investments.

New and better ways of being in the world are all around us and, when we raise our vibration, like attracts like. When my great friend Warren Stickney said he wants to help "ordinary people do extraordinary things," my soul soared to hear it, and no doubt your soul is soaring too. Warren went to high school with Barack Obama and is blessed with a beautiful boundless mind. He hopes to save politics (a bold mission), the world, and so many other things. We are both board members of The Wildlife Foundation, which is tasked with protecting the ecosystem of the United States, and helping endangered animals and plants. Our first project is an incredible ranch near Yellowstone National Park filled with bears, wolves, bison, and other wildlife.

New and better ways of being in the world are all around us.

My favorite quote from Warren is that his mission is to "activate solving problems, needs and adversity, by converting accidental philanthropy to lives of purpose and meaning." I see that as creating serendipitous purpose and meaning at the highest level, or put simply, "wrong roads, right destination."

If you have a dream, dare to follow it. Give it all the love and attention it needs. It may be a dream that lasts a handful of years, but don't be afraid to think big, to think beyond your lifetime. Who knows how long your idea might last. Did you know, for example, that kindergartens first appeared almost two hundred years ago? Now millions of children across the planet benefit from out-of-home care and play. The local kindergarten is where our kids can just be kids, with few rules, no homework, and lots of play.

Kindergarten, which literally means "garden for children," was founded by architect turned education pioneer, Friedrich Froebel. After a successful start in 1837, the Prussian government banned kindergartens in 1851. A year before he died, aged seventy, Froebel wrote to the King of Prussia:

> Do not allow the matter of childhood to become a tool of political parties . . . Therefore, I beg you again: Have the theory and practice of the Kindergarten examined and you will be convinced of its harmlessness if not of its benefits.

The ban was lifted nine years later, and eventually, one of Froebel's distant descendants ran one of the schools he had originally started. The rest is history.

This to me is a true visionary story. Some of us might start something that benefits many for one or two decades. Other possibilities last much, much longer, and Froebel's kindergartens are a perfect example of this. What's important is that we give our all to our projects that may last lifetimes—literally.

How is this possible? My friend Dave Erickson sent me Itzhak Bentov's book, *Stalking the Wild Pendulum: On the Mechanics of Consciousness.* I started reading the book at Chicago O'Hare International Airport, only to learn that Bentov had died shortly after takeoff from O'Hare, in a deadly plane crash that killed 271 people. This gave me cause to pause.

Reading on, I discovered that Bentov believes in the extension of life through our psyche. Put simply, he suggests that the collective information learned during one body's lifetime is available to us in future lives. In his words:

> I suggest that people having problems with accepting the concept of reincarnation consider this bundle of organized information as having continuity in time,

> while the physical body serves as just a temporary vehicle for the psyche. When the psyche, after having been without a physical body for a while (the period after death), decides that it needs additional pieces of information obtainable only through the physical body, it will acquire one and continue to associate with the new body until it wears out and dies.

I too believe that, through the grace and immense creativity of the universe, we are all on a journey of lifetimes, that we continue to return and grow and contribute, and that our single life work can outlast us. Why? Because we are living at an extraordinary time of human evolution.

I'm grateful to Dave also for the 2020 report from the Global Entrepreneur Development Institute that discusses how knowledge is evolving through technology, networks, and relationships, and how it is increasingly replacing physical capital and labor as the key driving force of economic growth.

It's exciting to see that it's individuals, rather than large firms, who are the leading factor in new knowledge creation. In short, real relationships and smaller, more tightly knit communities are creating higher levels of knowledge, impact, markets, ideas, companies, wealth, and systems. I like to think of these groups, including the company I helped start, as "Adult Kindergarten"—gardens for adults to think, act, play, and grow, just like children on their first day of school. Children who are not afraid to be spontaneous and curious.

Let our journey be an adventure in fulfillment, learning, and collective knowledge, long outlasting our death. Friedrich Froebel taught us this, first in life, and now more than 170 years later.

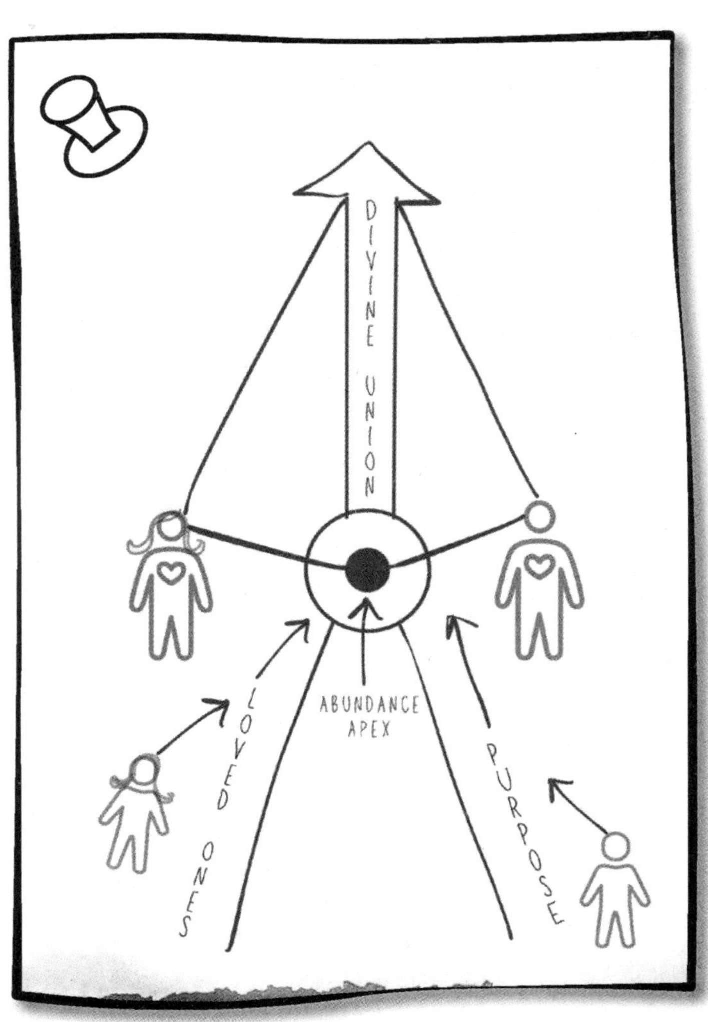
DIVINE UNION
ABUNDANCE APEX
LOVED ONES
PURPOSE

EPIC TAKEAWAYS

- ✓ Through the grace and immense creativity of the universe, we are all on a journey of lifetimes, and our single life work may well outlast us.
- ✓ To reach the Abundance Apex, you must rise through the most suffering, the most commitment, and the most effort.
- ✓ As we continue to strive to perfect the perfection in us, our hardships are transformed into our greatest soul pleasures.

12 DARE TO FOLLOW THE SIGNS

SO, WE'VE CONTEMPLATED TRUE ABUNDANCE, but how to get there? We land here on earth with a plan, a divinely inspired life map, which reveals itself to us over time, little by little. We don't get to see the whole map in one go, as it would be too overwhelming. We know when we've glimpsed a portion of our life map, because it electroshocks the soul, and activates our truest purpose.

As a child, I'd stare at maps for hours, mostly from *National Geographic*. Whether they were maps of Montana, Africa, Antarctica, India, the Himalayas, or ancient civilizations, of national parks or the galaxy, I loved those giant maps that took forever to unfold, then refold. One of my last remaining childhood possessions is a brownish globe, which I like to spin. I enjoy closing my eyes, then seeing where my finger lands when the spinning stops.

Maps are precious because they lay out the way ahead. Often, we can feel like we're marking time or treading through treacle, then we get to glimpse a new part of our life map, and immediately we feel more energized, clearer too, and more committed to following our true path. So, it's important we stay open. That way we're able to recognize those revelatory moments when the clouds part, and the way ahead becomes crystal clear.

I'd prayed for a trip to London, and later that day one of my friends invited me to attend an event there. A few hours later, while contemplating what this trip might mean, I was flipping through my dad's diary when I found a map of three cities: London, Paris, and Nancy (also in France). In that instant, everything—and I mean everything—stopped spinning, just like my globe. The path ahead was unmistakable; I almost dropped the diary. The word "Nancy" had remained in my consciousness after becoming acquainted with the work of Nancy Ann Tappe around indigo children. It had felt like there was a wider significance to it, and now here I was, staring at this map my father had left.

I just knew I had to follow this map drawn in February 1945. It meant I would have to travel first to London, then Paris, then on to Nancy. I let this sink in. It was then I decided I wouldn't stay in London or attend the event. London, it seemed, was just a place to start this journey within a journey. My soul sang to experience this moment of pure inspiration, which had landed directly in front of me, out of the blue.

I feel humbled to have an opportunity to follow my heart, to see where this soul journey leads. The pull to follow this map is so powerful (a clear sign of a higher calling), that suddenly I'm willing to leave everything and everyone, including my family. This shocks and excites me.

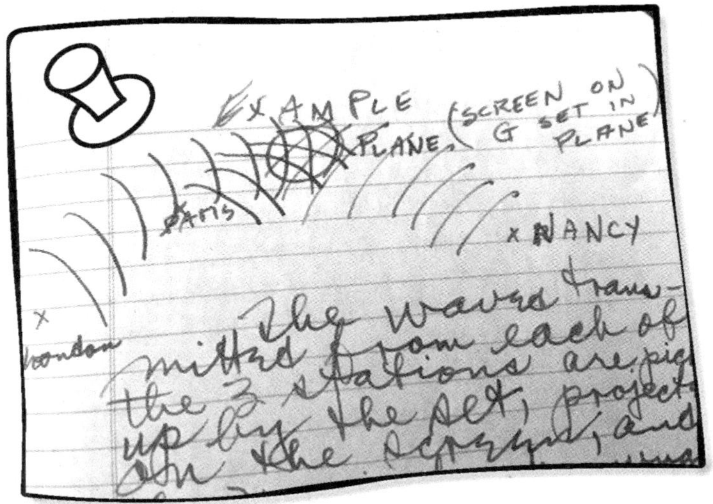

By always staying in the battle with ultimate bravery, honesty, and truth seeking, what was not sought becomes the ultimate destiny.

I note Dad drew the map joining London, Paris, and Nancy to illustrate the interplay of radar, receiving stations, and frequencies. From his simple drawing, I'm able to see how the waves are transmitted between the towers in these three European cities—transmissions that enable a bomber plane navigator to zero down on their target. A few pages later, Dad describes how he barely survived the mission the day after, with so many anti-aircraft shells aimed at his plane. I'm reminded sometimes, even when guided, the going can be tough. That, I know, is to test our resolve.

It's near impossible to grasp that someone seeing a simply drawn map on a piece of seventy-nine-year-old paper would be willing to risk everything they've built to follow this basic map. I've a wonderful life and then some, but when the Divine call comes, it's important we don't let the chance of a breakthrough slip through our fingers. Yes, this call to action feels scary, but that's how these deep callings often show up. To grow, we need to step out of our comfort zone. Welcome to visionary world for those not yet used to it! Already, I can feel the flak and shells exploding around me, as doubts creep in.

It's **so hard** to let go and just follow the call. It's really hard to step into the unknown, but this is what a deeply authentic life requires of everyone. The highest highs and the very lowest lows are all part of the experience. It's that willingness to suffer, to experience a breakthrough. There's very little space in between. You . . . just . . . keep . . . going . . . no . . . matter . . . what. This is how you become a shining example for others, a litmus test of true courage, strength, and insight for the people you serve. All else is pure hypocrisy.

As I think about the road ahead, I'm buoyed by insights from those who've gone before, reminding me to always stay in the battle. To be early, brave, and honest. This, I know, is my opportunity to open my heart wide in this moment, and in so doing I'm reminded that through this call, He that is Perfect is perfecting perfection in me. I do not want to lose everything for this journey, but I will do that, if that's what it requires.

I've learned that the only way to achieve the highest level of consciousness is through strategic patience, through great leadership suffering. This is how it's always been. Life's not always easy, but it is meant to be wonderful. And, as hard as soul journeys may be at times, there are always those who light the way. My great friend, Dana Weinberger, the first person to arrive at our company's first big in-person event, handed me a heart-shaped rock she'd held in her possession for thirty years. In that moment, Dana lit the way for me; I, in turn, am determined to hold that rock close wherever I go for the rest of my life.

The day before I sat down to share my soul journey here, Dana texted me saying:

> You will teach how to change the world, and why I truly love your energy is that it's of zero self-importance. I believe the reason it took you a while to see your path is because it's so strong. You weren't ready.

I treasure Dana's loving insights. I see now I **am** ready for whatever is asked of me, even though I've no idea what's going to happen on this soul journey I'm called to undertake. Grabbing a piece of paper, I draw my own version of this three-city map, a triangle because, as my ten-year-old Chase Breen reminds me, "Geometry unlocks consciousness."

Paying closer attention to the energetics of this trip, I discover London's motto is: *O Lord direct us.* For Paris, the City of Light, it's: *Someone wavers and does not sink.* If ever I doubted a Higher Power is directing me, I feel it now. I know that while there may be tricky moments ahead, I will not sink. I'm also heartened to know I'm not taking this epic journey alone. I know my purpose too. I'm seeking God, pure love, and light. And while I may waver at times, I remind myself that I will not sink.

A few days after seeing Dad's map, I'm introduced to Steven Gibson, an insightful entrepreneur, who wants to decentralize artificial intelligence. At the time Steven and I first talked, I had shared the map of my forthcoming soul journey with only a few very close friends, but I feel compelled to do so with Steven. There is something about his aura—indigo—and I know he'll understand.

As I tell Steven about the map and the London connection he smiles, indicating to his four-month adopted daughter on his lap. Her name, he explains, is London. Amazed, I stare down at

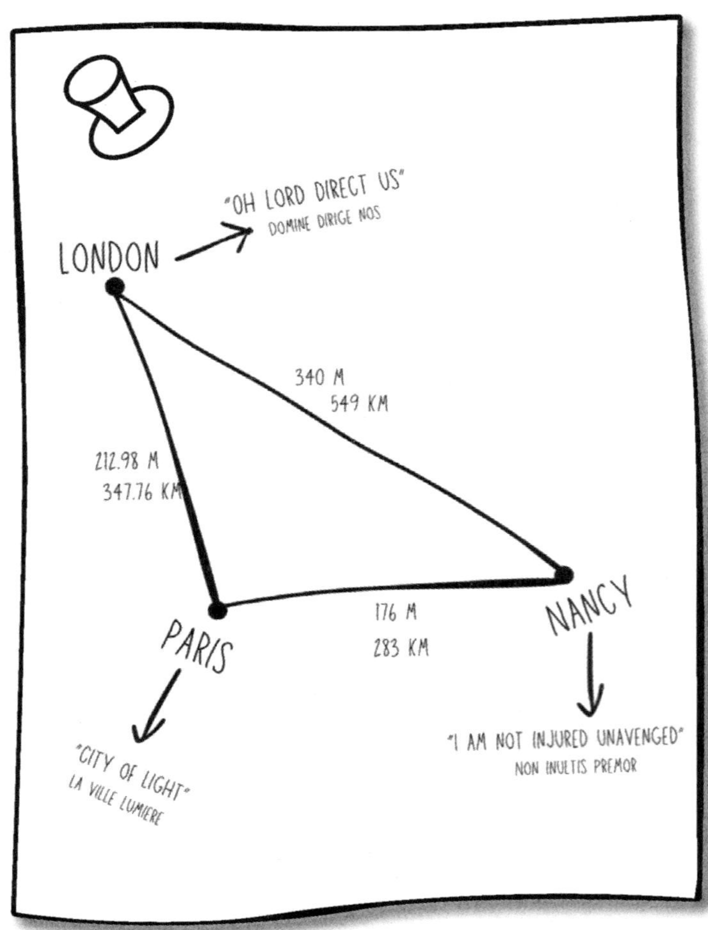
"OH LORD DIRECT US"
DOMINE DIRIGE NOS
LONDON
340 M
549 KM
212.98 M
347.76 KM
176 M
283 KM
PARIS
NANCY
"CITY OF LIGHT"
LA VILLE LUMIERE
"I AM NOT INJURED UNAVENGED"
NON INULTIS PREMOR

little London Gibson. Resting quietly on her dad's lap, she stares widely, as if in wonderment at the world, for the duration of our forty-five-minute conversation.

As I go on to tell Steven about Nancy, France, he says it's where his father was born, and where his grandfather had been a star soccer player for the city's professional team. Synchronicities piling on synchronicities! Logic, I've learned, can only take us so far. After that, the only true logic is illogic, love, and connectivity. Steven suggests that while in Nancy I visit the fountains in Stanislas Square. It's where his grandma's ashes are scattered. "I think you'll find massive inspiration there," he texts later.

As I contemplate my upcoming journey, I feel my ancestors drawing close. It's important to note that those who have gone before can also be our guides along the way, if we allow it. In recognizing this, my thoughts slip back to one the greatest, weirdest love stories ever.

As mentioned earlier, my dad Mike was fifty-seven and my mom Bonni was twenty-three when their lives intersected and glitched. They met after a drunk driver hit my father's car head-on and was killed instantly. Dad broke numerous bones and thought he was dead. When he woke up, he assumed Mom was his guiding angel. She was his nurse.

My grandmother died while Dad was in the hospital, which must have created unbearable pain for him. He'd taken care of his mother for decades, living with her after his dad died. I'm guessing that after my grandmother died, Dad had to find a new purpose, which was creating a family. The biggest glitch ever.

Mom and Dad didn't care what others thought. They created an exciting life for themselves and their three children. Mom had another boyfriend when she met Dad. She briefly married that boyfriend. Dad waited it out, following his intuition. Strategic patience at highest level.

As my journey approaches, I'm reminded of the importance of strategic patience, to help me access all the benefits of my mission. Recalling Steve's suggestion, I research the fountains in Nancy's main square, and discover they were built to honor Poseidon, God of the Sea, and his wife Amphitrite.

According to legend, when Poseidon first met Amphitrite, he was so lovestruck he knew he had to marry her. As God of the Sea, he could have married whoever he wanted, but he **really** wanted Amphitrite, the Goddess of Fertility. He immediately fell in love. Amphitrite fled to the farthest reaches of the world, hiding in the Atlas Mountains that separate the Sahara and the Mediterranean Sea. By the way, don't forget "atlas" is a collection of maps. It always goes back to maps!

Poseidon was patient (remember, patience means "suffering"). He sent several creatures with gifts to find her. The creature that convinced Amphitrite to accept Poseidon was a dolphin named Delphinus, who was in turn rewarded with a star constellation named after him. Amphitrite and Poseidon went on to have two or three children, and are remembered through time in numerous paintings, murals, temples, and other artifacts.

With the themes of love and destiny fresh in my mind, I speak with my great friend Jake Merriman, who likes to think way out of the box, and whose latest company delivers an incredible meditation program called Mahalo, a Hawaiian word meaning thanks, gratitude, admiration, praise, esteem, regards, or respect. Jake and I tend talk once a month, and he really is a merry man, a kind, loving soul who is creating massive transformation for the world. Jake travels widely, and when we talked, he was in Greece, living for a few months on the island Tinos.

When I tell him about Nancy and the fountains, Jake says that a couple of days ago he'd talked to his travel agent about what to do

on Tinos, and was told he must visit the Sanctuary of Poseidon and Amphitrite. Apparently, Tinos is the only island in the Cyclades group of islands that has an entire temple dedicated to Poseidon and his wife, the sea nymph Amphitrite.

Because of this temple, in times past Tinos was a significant religious center. Many would come to the temple to purify themselves, when first arriving on the island. When the temple was reconstructed, it became a haven for the persecuted. Made of local marble, it was decorated with Poseidon's symbols, including dolphins and tridents. Sadly, once Christianity was established, the temple was destroyed.

After a lifetime of feeling and thinking, and finally while writing this sentence, I realize this book is my Delphinus. I'm dedicated to pursuing and attracting my Amphitrite, my feminine principle, and all the Amphitrites of the world—those willing make our precious planet more fertile, to create the glitches and disruptions, and to bring about much-needed rebirths and evolutions.

EPIC TAKEAWAYS

- ✓ Have you found your true love? If not, what's stopping you?
- ✓ Where do you find inspiration? In a particular place, inside yourself, or elsewhere?
- ✓ Discover strength in your parents' love story, or other love stories.

A LIFE EXHILAFIED

TODAY IT'S ALL HAPPENING. I'm heading to Iceland on a stopover to London. I've always wanted to go there, and now it's happening. Earlier today, I received great direction from the inimitable Melissa Bernstein who, with her husband Doug, founded Melissa & Doug, the world's number one brand of wooden toys for preschoolers.

Melissa is like I am, a boundless mind; Doug is like my Sarah, a stabilizer. Needing to turn her anxiety and extreme depression into creativity, Melissa helped start their company thirty-five years ago. Inspired by Douglas Horton, the late American Protestant clergyman and academic leader, Melissa follows his motto: *Action cures fear. Inaction creates terror*.

Melissa has battled anxiety and depression most of her life. She's one of the most brilliant people ever. There's a reason why Melissa & Doug is the world's number one wooden toy brand, and it starts with Melissa's vision to transform trauma into triumph, by creating a rainbow of wondrous toys. Melissa explains this to me:

> Channeling darkness into light through making toys that could elicit joy in children was lifesaving for me. Today, I've come to understand that I don't create solely out of darkness, but out of the entire spectrum of emotion—from the highest of highs and peaks of ecstasy, all the way down to the bowels of despair and abyss of nothingness. I love the word "indiscriminate" because it means done at random and without careful judgment . . . isn't that the way life should be? Who wants to be measured and careful? Boring!

Melissa is the best one-liner wordsmith I've come across. Her life mantra is: *Step on out of the head and move into the heart, free to channel all dread into jubilant art!* She continues to explain:

> The jubilant part is the key to this practice, [and is] based on my [former] belief that I could only channel darkness (existential nihilism and an acute sense of meaninglessness) into more darkness, that I could never positively touch anyone or anything.

Melissa's goal is to live each day "exhilafied"—a potent mix of exhilaration and terror.

Exhilafied is how I feel right now as I set off on this strange soul journey. I can't tell you how exhilarated I am. Everything is aligning so beautifully—like an elegant Melissa & Doug toy. I am so grateful for this opportunity. Yet I am also **terrified**. Come to think of it, I've never been this scared in my life. Not even before Jake and Chase were born. This is a different kind of scared.

What if there's nothing to be found in Nancy? Yet somehow, I know deep within that there will be something transcendent.

I'm reminded again of the article on Kazimierz Dabrowski that Melissa sent me recently. Dabrowski liked to talk of "overexcitabilities"—abundant emotional, intellectual, and imaginational lives. Or, as Melissa describes them: "Rocket boosters in one's soul that propel us forward, despite our hardships and challenges."*

Everything in me feels charged to see how much has aligned so far, almost like a symphony. Now, as I hop on a plane with no hotel booked, no cash, and nothing else in my possession besides some clothes, a passport, credit card, the heart-shaped rock that Dana Weinberger gave me exactly a week ago, and this laptop computer, my attention turns to my gray hat with a yellow-eyed black raven on it.

Raven. Totems. Not to be ignored. Not if you're in search of additional guidance. Raven is my Native American spirit animal. It approaches signaling transition, change, and healing. How appropriate it is that Raven accompanies me on this epic soul journey. I feel in a space of transition and know in my soul it comes offering me change and healing.

I'm humbled to be reminded that the universe places plentiful signposts on our path, if we can but recognize them. I saw a raven in California when I was running in the sunshine along the Pacific Ocean a few months back. The raven was on top of a cliff staring into the ocean, just observing. Raven's presence felt like a benediction, and it does again. Immediately, I'm flooded with a sense of real blessing.

The only other item I've brought on the journey is Dad's diary. I don't care about material things. If our house was burning down, I'd save Sarah and the kids (they'd probably save me), our three dogs,

* Jenny Grant Rankin, PhD, "The Overexcitabilities High-IQ People May Have," *Psychology Today*, August 13, 2025, https://www.psychologytoday.com/au/blog/much-more-than-common-core/202412/the-overexcitabilities-high-iq-people-have.

and Dad's diary. I don't care about anything else. It's just a house. You can have a home anywhere. I never, ever take the diary out of our house, but I'm doing so for this trip. I need Dad and his words from the toughest battle of his life with me for this pilgrimage of sorts.

This is the point on my epic journey where I wade into deeper waters, where I seize the courage to step out, not knowing where I'm being led. Why? Because by this point on a soul journey, yours or mine, having set off, we enter into a much deeper relationship with ourselves and our purpose, with what we're capable of, and a deeper relationship with those around us. Put simply, I'm now connected into the web of life on a whole new level, and from this elevated standpoint anything is possible.

My journey is one now of faith—a belief that in daring to follow the threads life has placed in my path, I will reap profound benefits for myself and others. All that's required of me now is that I remain present to the signs, the nuances, and the insights awaiting me.

The process of travel can be simply a matter of getting oneself from A to B. Sometimes that's all that's required of us. But if we make every journey about the destination, along the way we miss very powerful insights and ideas, new or more refined ways of being in the world.

Landing here in Iceland's capital, Reykjavik, I've made it across the Atlantic after a beautiful overnight flight from Chicago. What a magical country! Iceland is special. It's amazing anyone or anything can live here. Yet it was someone's dream, someone's inspiration, and here it is to inspire others. Sometimes we can talk ourselves out of possibilities before we've given them a chance. Not so the boundless mind.

There are only about 350,000 Icelandic people, and remarkably, this nation lives among glaciers and ice caves, geysers and volcanos, hot springs, and waterfalls. In fact, they don't just live here; they've found a way to thrive. A great life lesson for the rest of us about vision and intent. The Vikings, who came here over 1,200 years ago from Scandinavia, must have endured unbearable, yet somehow survivable, conditions—kind of like being an entrepreneur, or a change agent for the greater good. They were warriors, and we can be too. No excuses. Period. These thick-bearded visionary settlers built a foundation that has created arguably the coolest country on the planet.

Those Vikings brought with them their horses, the amazing Icelandic Horse, which I learn about as the sun comes up and the plane is about to land. Some of these remarkable horses have blue eyes. Since their arrival in the country, this breed has remained virtually unchanged. Iceland's brutal weather doesn't affect these amazing creatures. These small, pony-sized horses have a gait Icelanders call *tölt*, where three of their legs touch the ground at the same time, and another gait known as a "flying pace."

More importantly, when looked at as a totem or symbol, the Icelandic Horse is closely associated with fertility. Is the Icelandic Horse signaling a fertile time ahead? I feel intuitively this is so, that I'm undergoing a potent preparation as I step into a new life cycle. That, after all, is what soul journeys are about. If we heed the call, they fill us up, expand our vision, so we can serve ourselves and others more effectively.

The universe converses with us constantly, but sadly, we rarely take note. We get busy, distracted, and, because we haven't learned to read the signs, we fail to sniff the wind. What I do sense in this moment is that I'm being put on notice here. Horse has always had a profound place in the shaman's view of the world, as Horse pulls the sun and moon chariot. It lights up the world with its mane. These symbols are powerful. I need to ponder what the sun and moon might mean, what lights up my world.

If we want to live and think outside the box, we need to hold a new and wider vision. To access this wider vision, it helps to learn to recognize and read the signposts around us. When we do, we get to see further, travel further, with greater speed and insight. But remember, the universe never wastes energy, and nor should we.

The Icelandic Horse has been protected, loved, and honored by Icelandic people, starting with their original Viking brothers and sisters. The same cannot be said for many racehorses across the world. My great friend Pavla Nygaard is trying to solve this problem with her genius heart and brain, and rocket scientist husband. Her mission is to transform the horse-racing industry through ethical practice. "I believe that we don't choose our passions," Pavla says. "They choose us, and it's up to us to honor them. Their [the horses'] pure visual and spiritual beauty has inspired me as much as it has inspired painters, sculptors, architects, writers, musicians, filmmakers, and legends for centuries," she adds. I agree. We need to take better care of those who serve us, and those we share the planet with.

Leaving Iceland, I arrive in London. I've had no sleep for the past thirty hours. I used to live like this back in my teens and twenties, but haven't done so for decades. I'm glad to be in this lack-of-sleep state right now, as I'm hyper aware of what's happening around me. I look at a newspaper, then another, another, and another, waiting for a train to Paris.

I used to work in newspapers and was a full-time journalist for twenty years, before entrepreneur life chose me. Honestly, I'd forgotten that too often the corporate world is the opposite of true abundance. As I look at the theme of countless newspaper headlines, telling of outrage, risk, war, nightmare, disaster, scandal, and persecution, the word that seems to sum up all this energy for me is "shame." According to Dr. David Hawkins's Scale of Consciousness, shame is the absolute lowest level anyone alive can reach. To give you some idea of what this means, shame is listed at 20, whereas full consciousness is 1,000.

I guess another word that sums up all this negativity is "sadness." It's just so sad that this type of material is shared every single day with billions of people across the world, who are just looking to know what's happening in their communities large and small. It's unfortunate to come to London, one of the world's grandest cities, and have these headlines and articles sit here in the newsstands and in the coffee shops, piled up on tables or wherever else you can see them. It is pure toxicity—a toxicity we're best to avoid.

It's easy to understand why so many people are so negative so much of the time. They're just not aware of the impact of what they're seeing. Awareness, by contrast, is extremely high on the Scale of Consciousness (700). Dr. Hawkins noted in his research only about 1 percent of the world reaches Inner Love (500) on the Consciousness Scale. The next state, Oneness (540), is achieved by 0.4 percent of the world. Almost no one is fully aware, so we all need to work hard to change that.

Now on the Underground (subway) ride from Heathrow Airport to St. Pancras international train station, I meet Tarek, a Slovakian who's lived in London for six years. Tarek has just returned from a long trip to Canada, where he saw big brown grizzly bears and bright white mountain goats. Tarek works for a company as a marketer and owns a bakery with five employees. He says that after two years, his bakery is starting to turn a profit. I asked him what his first name meant. He didn't know. So, we looked it up together.

Tarek comes from the Arabic word *Tariq*, which means morning star. It's this energy of newness the world needs right now, and the energy of the morning star, that I choose to embrace on this my strange soul journey. Ours was just a fifteen-minute conversation.

Tarek did most of the talking, which is fine. I prefer it that way. You can learn a lot from people just by asking them a nice question and listening kindly. Conscious conversations uplift the planet.

Once you've mastered the rules, then you must ***reject*** *everything you know*
and start over again with a completely blank slate.
You must bring yourself to the domain and see it with completely new eyes.
That space is where novelty is conceived.

Melissa Bernstein, entrepreneur and creative

I arrive in Paris, my favorite city. I could live here the rest of my life, walking the streets and eating warm croissants covered in butter, but I can't be distracted. I'm here to find my truest soul purpose. So, I immediately hop on a train to Nancy, having traveled thousands upon thousands of miles without sleep. Carrying Dad's World War II diary back to Europe with me, and reading it while returning to where he fought, is beyond spiritual for me. For a good part of the train ride, I just read his diary. It feels nothing short of a miracle to be doing what I'm doing. I strongly resonate with Melissa Bernstein's thoughts about rejecting everything you know and starting over again with a completely blank slate.

On the train I hold Dad's diary close. It is dark brown, with *Record* on the cover. I see the word is from Old French meaning "remembrance" from the Latin *cor* or "cord," both of which mean "heart." To me, my journey is actually an inner "war diary." For all those wanting to change the world for good, we need to do an inner battle with those parts of ourselves that need transforming. I share this thought in a WhatsApp entrepreneur group, and my insightful friend Simone Rosati adds, "Remembrance = reunification of different parts of the body. **Memory** has a spiritual function in us . . . individually and collectively. Enjoy this **treasure** from your dad."

Around 9:15 p.m., I reach Nancy. About fifteen minutes later, I see the fountains I was directed to just as the sun sets. Remarkable! About four hours after that, I wake from a deep sleep and solve the riddle. A few minutes later, my great warrior, my Amphitrite, texted me that her heart had been broken. I spent the next several hours on the phone with her to make sure her beautiful, ethereal soul was OK.

I thought this book would be about the Eiffel Tower, but I was wrong. I didn't even see Eiffel's masterpiece on this trip. I find a much more sacred place in Nancy. Serendipity strikes its lightning glitch again as I'm drawn back to Dad diary, to First Lt. Mike Breen's account of the Battle of Hürtgen Forest across Germany and Belgium:

> This is it. All that has gone before, the training, the studying, the discomforts, the irritations all take a back seat now. . . . From now on, it's the payoff. Here starts the distinction between the petty discomforts of training and the extreme and acute sufferings of actual war . . . Here is where you find out what it really means to be miserable, to be so damn cold, wet and hungry that you just don't give a damn about anything . . . But there are compensations. You are amongst **real men.** You see them fight, kill, get wounded, and get killed. You see competent men giving all they've got and a helluva lot more, and you're one of them.

It's May 22, 2024, and I'm sitting in an ultra-small hotel room four floors up in this stunning French city. I've just opened the balcony window. It's 11:06 a.m. The sun is out. I've seen several ravens already—transition, change, healing. Not surprised. Across the street there's a restaurant called La Camaraderie (friendship). On the other side is a dining establishment, Transparence. Strange, every cell feels a call to greater authenticity and transparency.

About a hundred yards to the east is Place Stanislas—the holiest place I've ever seen. It's pure sanctuary. When the time comes, I think I'll have my ashes spread here, like Steven Gibson's grandmother. Dad, I realize, was a genius. The map he drew that guided me here. I promised my father I'd follow his map. It's such a blessing. It has led me on a path of many revelations large and small. Already I can feel them moving within and around me, transforming me. I start crying uncontrollably. Dad's legacy will live forever. He was my best friend. It broke my heart when he died.

Many battles, I learn, have been fought in Nancy. It's a gorgeous city, gridded and ancient and absolutely spectacular. At the center of its heart in Place Stanislas, in honor of the eighteenth-century King Stanislaus I, is this Polish king's statue. Interestingly, here is the heart within the heart of the sanctuary. The core within the core. On the statue's north face, there is in translation: *To Stanislas the Benefactor, Lorraine [is] grateful.* My soul sings to be reminded that a grateful heart creates an abundance mindset, an exponential network, limitless opportunities, and more besides.

The King Stanislaus statue points toward the fountains and statues in the square's northwest and northeast corners. To the northeast is Poseidon, who searched the earth for the one he loved, holding his massive trident toward the northwest, where the object of his love, the beautiful Amphitrite, resides. This is one grateful triangular partnership between a King, the God of the Sea, and the God-woman loved at first sight. A beautiful example of pure +2s. And, as all great triangular partnerships must have, one corner has

A
STANISLAS
LE BIENFAISANT
LA
LORRAINE
RECONNAISSANTE
1831

feminine energy to balance the melting masculine ego.

Geometry, I'm reminded, unlocks consciousness. Thank you, Chase Breen. You and your lightning-fast brother Jake are great warriors, like your ancestors. And here, at the core within the core, is where the riddle is answered. When I wake up, I immediately realize why I am here, not only in Nancy, but on earth at this time.

The hotel where I'm staying is Les Portes D'Or—the Golden Doors. It was booked on the train about twenty minutes before arriving in Nancy, as I needed a place to sleep. Surrounding Place Stanislas is a magnificent hotel, an opera house, restaurants, a nightclub, art museum, and arcs, similar to the Arc de Triomphe in Paris, along with endless bright gold-painted gates. It's beyond spectacular. Heavenly, really. There are dozens of female and male masked statues staring into the seventeen-acre square, almost seeming to judge anyone that comes in through the Place Stanislas's gates.

And now, the answer to the riddle. Stanislaus does not look or point to the southwest or southeast of the square. There are no statues in these corners, only empty gates allowing people in. There are no +2 souls firmly in place to unlock consciousness and the Four Elements. The king has turned his back on the other half of the square, literally.

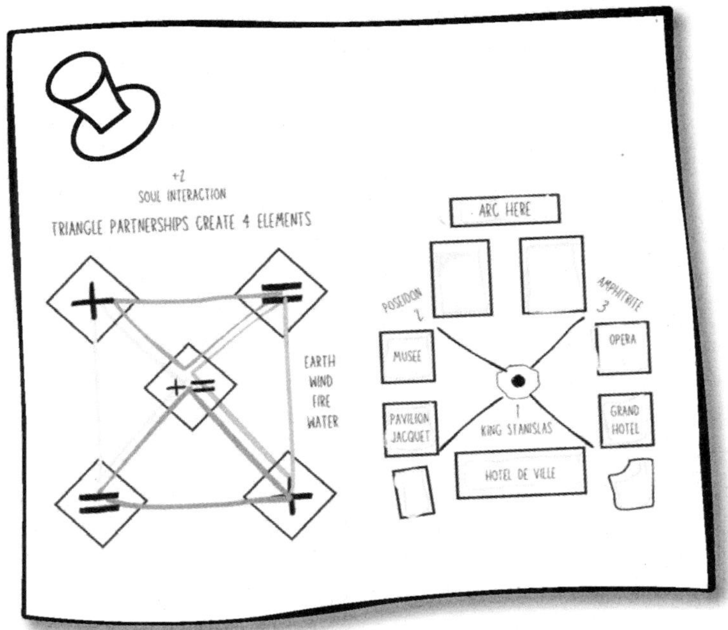

Four Elements drawn on April 18, 2024. Map of Place Stanislas added May 22.

When I was originally drawing the Four Elements, my brilliant friend Beth Kraszewski was sitting a few feet away in a Strategic Coach® session. As I finished the drawing, she texted me a book recommendation, *The Four Agreements* by Don Miguel Ruiz, which features a cover very similar to my Four Elements drawing. I see the world as a missing piece of +2s, not fulfilling their duty as +2s, and failing to fill their rightful spots in the southwest and southeast corners of Place Stanislas. With the Four Elements incomplete, the world lacks wholeness. We each need to complete the Four Agreements within ourselves.

The Four Agreements ask that we:

1. Be impeccable with our word.
2. Don't take anything personally.
3. Don't make assumptions.
4. Always do our best.

We can't hope for a fully aligned world, when most of us aren't aligned with our true selves. This is a profound understanding. I've traveled thousands of miles to see and comprehend this. Guided by an old hand-drawn map, by light bearers I've met along the way, by potent totems, and by sacred geometry, I'm able to connect all the dots, to touch the core within the core. To glimpse the ultimate, pure heart of hearts.

As I contemplate the potency of sacred geometry, I'm reminded that the human heart has four chambers, two upper and two lower. The upper chambers receive incoming blood. The lower chambers pump the blood out around the body, infusing it with life and nourishment.

The Four Elements and +2 Soul Interaction drawing also has those four chambers, which reflect the map of Nancy's geometric core. The tragedy of what we're witnessing now in the world is a **broken heart** that's not pumping out its blood to feed and nourish. Blood is going everywhere. Countless opportunities are being lost, individually and globally. The toxicity of the press I witnessed in London, and the many dark acts we're witnessing across our tiny jewel of a planet, is a symptom of this brokenness.

I see the solution in one of two ways. You can seek your true soul and truest purpose by living life like King Stanislaus I, Poseidon, and Amphitrite—and obviously that doesn't mean you literally have to be a king or a god. Or you can choose a lesser life, one that fails to nourish and inspire you, let alone those around you. So, you either go for it, or you don't and continue to make excuses. The headlines from the London papers are the result of so many people not taking the leap.

To heal and honor the world, you must heal and honor yourself, starting by honoring a Higher Power. You must find your core within the core, then heal your broken heart, to allow it to pump fully through all four chambers. That's the answer. It's the one and only answer. Let the maps, and all the many signposts and luminaries who guided me on this journey, guide you. I risked everything to take this soul journey. It has rebuilt my broken heart. It was well worth the effort to honor a Higher Power, and my dad too, and every light bearer along the way who has led me to this moment.

Months after finishing the first draft of this book, a friend and member of our network, Anthony Englert, recommended that our group read *Autobiography of a Yogi* by Paramahansa Yogananda. This book has been named one of the top 100 spiritual books of the last century. Reading the book, then listening to Paramahansa's meditations, I am in no doubt that the best way to heal a broken heart is by honoring a Higher Power. I recite this passage every day, while running in the early morning under a bright full moon:

> He [God] is playing hide-and-seek with His devotees, but some day, after this play is over, to each one of you He will say: "I hid from you long, not to torture you, but to make our reunion in the end bright and beautiful. After your search of incarnations, you have come at last to Me, and I joyfully welcome you to your Home. I have been waiting long for you. You were not the only one who was seeking. Through all your life's experiences it was I, wearing disguises of different loves of family and friends, who pursued you. I have been watching and waiting for you more eagerly than

> you have sought Me. Many times, you forgot Me, but I could not forget you, My child. Beloved, of your own free will you have at last come back to Me. We shall never again be parted."

This too has helped me connect in with that Higher Power. It's an ongoing journey. Though at times it has been tortuous to reach this point, it's so worth it.

I opened this final chapter with the diary entry from Dad about going into combat, because that's what your soul journey is: an all-out battle to heal your heart. This is the biggest battle of your life. It's the only battle that matters. The question is: Do you want to be one of the ones who will heal their hearts and embrace true greatness—or not?

Do take the soul journey you're called to. Look for the signs around you. I just had to listen to Dad, my family, visionaries around me, and, of course, my own heart and intuition. And, without Sarah's ultimate loving support, I would have floated away a long time ago. She is pure harmony and joy. She will always be that way—no matter what happens.

I'm praying—really, really praying—that this journey inspires you to find your soul and purpose, and to follow it wherever it takes you, no matter what. The world needs you to do this, because we are here to seek, to fulfill our destiny. Because every intentional journey we take has the capacity to profoundly impact our soul destiny. And every word has a meaning. Every . . . single . . . word.

It took me many, many lifetimes to find my true soul and truest purpose. After failing this final exam many times, I hope I've finally passed the test.

This epic journey is now complete. Let the next one begin.

I am grateful. Be well. +=

THE AFTERWORD

JUST EIGHTY-SIX MINUTES AFTER REALIZING WHY I had traveled all the way to Nancy, France, Mom sent me a quick text message that read, *I wrote Normy today. My father was apparently married after the Korean War and helped raise two children. One of them is Norm. My family has always wondered whether my dad was Norm or Norm's brother's biological father.*

My mom finally decided to see if it was true and messaged Norm, who has always denied this.

I met Norm at dinner with my dad and younger brothers when I was really young. We talked about baseball. The only other thing I remember was that Norm had similar thick dark brown hair to me and Dad. Also, he's an attorney, just like Dad. If Norm is indeed my biological half-brother, I hope to see him again soon and show him this journey about the man who helped raise him and me. And I'd love to hear some of his stories about my/our dad as well.

A month later, I found out that Norm was **not** my half-brother, but his older brother almost certainly was. One of my much-older first cousins sent me a detailed history of my father's first wife, including of the older son, who they almost certainly created while they were married. My cousin sent me a photo of my father, grandmother, and the two boys Dad helped raise, well before I was born. Yet another mending of the heart. What incredible serendipity.

What grace to allow broken connections to be mended.

As my heart fills to a new level, I'm even more committed to creating a +2 planet that honors the presence of a Higher Power in our lives. To do this, I know I need support. I put out this request for further guidance to the universe, then received a text message during our company's in-person event, which included only +2s who were healing and honoring themselves first, so they could heal and honor the world.

This message came from Rajesh Setty, a key connection point to Dr. Chopra, author of nineteen books. Rajesh texted that the partnership with Dr. Chopra was almost certainly going to happen.

When we dare to embrace our soul's destiny, miracles happen.

ABOUT THE AUTHOR

JUSTIN BREEN is the founder and CEO of the global PR firm BrEpic Communications and the exclusive connectivity platform BrEpic Network. His first book, *Epic Business,* was a bestseller in six countries. Breen started BrEpic Communications in 2017 and launched BrEpic Network in 2022. He has built an international network of extraordinary people and believes strongly in the power of introductions and creating important relationships. Breen is an active member of the Strategic Coach 10x Ambition Program and the Abundance 360 Summit, and he mentors countless emerging entrepreneurs. He lives in the Chicago suburbs with his wife, Dr. Sarah Breen; their epic sons, Jake and Chase; and their dogs, Dr. Pepper and Toffee Kisses.